VX: A Deadly Mist

by

C. B. Murray

authorHOUSE™
1663 Liberty Drive, Suite 200
Bloomington, Indiana 47403
(800) 839-8640
www.AuthorHouse.com

This book is a work of fiction. Places, events, and situations in this story are purely fictional and any resemblance to actual persons, living or dead, is coincidental.

First published by AuthorHouse 10/04/04

ISBN: 1-4184-9229-9 (sc)
ISBN: 1-4184-9230-2 (dj)

Printed in the United States of America
Bloomington, Indiana

This book is printed on acid-free paper.

ACKNOWLEDGEMENTS

My heartfelt thanks goes to my husband and best friend Richard Murray, for his encouragement, support and editing of the various stages of this book. My appreciation to Ada Koch for the idea of the cover of the book and for her reading of the manuscript and suggestions of plot. Grateful acknowledgement to Stanley Sandler for alerting me to the hazards of chemical warfare and to both Stanley Sandler and John Carberry for technical advice on chemical agents.

DEDICATION

To Richard, Ada and Annette

TABLE OF CONTENTS

ACKNOWLEDGEMENTS v

DEDICATION vii

PROLOGUE xi

CHAPTER ONE 1

CHAPTER TWO 9

CHAPTER THREE 23

CHAPTER FOUR 35

CHAPTER FIVE 49

CHAPTER SIX 61

CHAPTER SEVEN 73

CHAPTER EIGHT 83

CHAPTER NINE 93

CHAPTER TEN 103

CHAPTER ELEVEN 115

CHAPTER TWELVE 127

READING GROUP QUESTIONS AND TOPICS FOR DISCUSSION 137

PROLOGUE

Chemical weapons have a long history, starting in the 4th century BC when the Athenians lost their fort to the allies of the Spartans. The Boethians forced the Athenians out with heavy chemical smoke. Then in 660 A.D. Kalinkos, thought to be a Syrian alchemist, invented Greek fire. The lost formula probably consisted of resin, pitch, sulfur, naphtha, lime and saltpeter. Since it floated on water and set fire to ships, it was a super naval weapon. Many Americans remember the Germans' use of mustard agent in World War I when mustard-filled artillery shells killed 90,00 men and maimed over a million. Though chemical weapons were repugnant, countries continued to use them: the Japanese in Manchuria and Italians in Ethiopia in the '30s, the Egyptians against Yemen in'63, the Russians in Afghanistan, Iraq first against Iran and then against the Kurds in the '80s and '90s. While chemical weapons were never used in World War II, a U.S. Liberty ship, the S.S. John Harvey, carrying bombs loaded with mustard agent was blown up in the harbor at Bari, Italy. An unknown number of civilians and 600 service men died from the mustard-laden smoke from the explosion. A more recent terrorist use of chemical warfare was the Sarin attack in a Tokyo subway in 1995.

In 1925 The Geneva Protocol was drafted outlawing the first use of biological or chemical warfare. Eighty nations voted to ratify the Protocol. Three nations voted against the Protocol: Australia, Portugal and the United States. On April 29, 1997 the U.S. ratified the Chemical Weapons Convention; 179 nations have signed it, 157 nations have ratified it, though 16 countries have not signed it. The Chemical Weapons Convention (CWC) prohibits the development, production, stockpiling and use of chemical weapons. The Organization for the Prohibition of Chemical Weapons (OPCW) in The Hague was established to be responsible for implementation of CWC by the year 2007. At the time of the ratification the U. S. declared 62,559,480 pounds and Russia 80,000,000 pounds of chemical weapons.

The chemical agents used in weapons today are categorized as either nerve, blood, blister, choking, psychological or harassing agents. Those found most in stockpiles are the blister agents (mustard and lewisite) and nerve agents (Sarin and VX). The nerve agents are refinements of insecticide production. While often called gases, they are really liquids with boiling points ranging from 158°C to 298°C.

The nerve agents Sarin (GB) and VX are organophosphates. In the body, a chemical, acetycholine, stimulates muscle action. An enzyme AChE inhibits acetycholine so muscles can rest. The nerve agents in chemical weapons block the action of the enzyme AChE so acetycholine keeps on stimulating the muscles, resulting in convulsions, coma and death in more drastic instances. The effects on a person depend on many factors: how much is used, where it enters the body, when treatment is applied, physical condition of the person, temperature, etc. Small amounts of nerve agents are lethal. For instance: 2 mg of Sarin (GB) inhaled is toxic, 10 mg of VX on the skin is toxic. For size, compare this to an aspirin tablet weighing 325 mg. Two drugs are used as antidotes: atropine and pralidoxine. Kits called Mark I containing these drugs are given to army personnel and anyone working with the chemical agents.

In keeping with the CWC, the U.S. Army and its contractors have begun destruction of the chemical stockpiles under the Resource Conservation and Recovery Act (RCRA). Two methods are being used, (1) incineration and (2) chemical neutralization followed by either bio-oxidation or further aqueous oxidation followed by bio-oxidation depending on the chemical agent. Controlled incineration has been used to destroy chemical agents and has proved efficient. Citizen groups have been vocal in resisting the use of incineration in highly populated areas, so the government is experimenting with chemical neutralization. Of course, once the chemical weapons are neutralized, then the plants where this was done will have to be neutralized, since they are now contaminated. The U.S. has begun its chemical agent destruction process and lists the percentage agent destroyed, munitions destroyed and the construction status of chemical weapon disposal facilities. Russia has completed only 3% of the disposal facilities at its Shchurch'ye, Russia facility. The U.S. had been helping the Russian project financially.

The U.S. began Sarin production in 1950's and VX in the early 60's. In addition to bulk one-ton containers holding these materials, the U.S. has chemical agents in 50-year old munitions: M55 rockets, land mines, 500 to 750 pound bombs, spray tanks, 105mm, 155mm., and 8-inch projectiles. The U.S. Army lists eight sites where chemical weapons are stockpiled. These are: Tooele, Utah; Umatilla, Oregon; Anniston, Alabama; Pine Bluff, Arkansas; Newport, Indiana; Aberdeen, Maryland; Pueblo, Colorado and Blue Grass, Kentucky. All the munitions on Johnston Island in the Pacific have been destroyed. In addition to the stockpiled weapons mentioned above, there is a group labeled nonstockpiled weapons, some of which are located on the sites listed and some are buried and forgotten. Some of the non-stockpile materials are listed in army records and for some the records have been lost.

All stockpile sites, their history, how to find them, maps of the layout of the sites, their buildings' locations and contents, information and forms to fill out to apply for entrance to the site, and names of personnel are listed on the internet. While heavily guarded, are these sites impenetrable? Few things in today's world are.

CHAPTER ONE

"So what did Dudley have to say?" Chloe leaned back in the leather wing chair by the fireplace and studied John Davis, the slouching young man seated opposite. A cell phone dangled from his hand. The late afternoon light from the tall living room windows deepened the lines of the scowl on his face. A rumpled newspaper lay on the floor where he had thrown it when the phone rang.

John turned half way in his chair with exaggerated effort and complained, "He wants to come by and walk with me to Hanson's bar for a drink. He was very explicit that we walk and that we not have a drink here by the blazing fire. He sounded so damned mysterious and nervous. Can you think of anything more aggravating then going out on a misty, foggy fall day when you could be so comfortable here? If he hadn't sounded so damned upset, I would have told him to bug off!"

Chloe scanned the tall figure clad in impeccable gray flannel pants and cashmere sweater and laughed. "You sound like an old man. Cozy by the fire! Want a shawl or a rocker?"

"Okay! Point taken." He stood up and stretched. "I mean we're going to see him tomorrow at the meeting Don Mozley from the

State Department has set up. Remember Don has been working with Homeland Security. He's asking for the Noir's help and since you are the senior member of our group," he paused and smiled wickedly over the word 'senior', "you're coming to that too, right? So why couldn't it wait? Why walk?" John negotiated the loafers he had kicked under the chair and balancing on one foot tried to regroup.

Chloe sat a little straighter, "Well now, that is odd. Why indeed would he want to meet with you now? Perhaps this is a personal problem. And why walk unless he's afraid of an electronic bug in the car?" She laughed. "Is your car or house bugged, John?"

"My dear Chloe, can you honestly think the owner of some the most successful computer gadget companies in the country, the promoter of every electronic marvel under the sun, would permit his car or home to be bugged? Now if it were your lovely granddaughter who had called and asked to walk, I would have been out the door right now waiting for her to appear, hat in hand along with flowers and champagne! By the way, where is Gabriel now? The last I heard she was in Paris with her formidable father."

"Well, I bring you good news on this rainy day." Chloe laughed. "They called last night. Gabriel and Rene are coming to Washington on some government business. They plan to stay here in town, but visit Richard at his plantation out on the Potomac. Did you know Richard had a plantation? His grandfather left it to him."

John's smile immediately turned to a frown and he started to scowl again. "Oh, yes, I remember. The righteous Richard Moore who can do no wrong, whom all women adore, including my lovely Gabriel. What would be more appropriate then a gorgeous plantation on the Potomac? I take it the place is huge and filled with valuable antiques?"

Chloe nodded. "As a matter of fact, it is large and filled with exquisite antiques from his family. But I don't know what you're worried about. Your family has a mansion in every city here and abroad! I don't think you have to worry about Richard's single state much longer, either. Have you seen him and Harriet together lately? You know, you could invite Gabriel and Rene to stay here. Rene no longer blames me for his wife's death, so they might stay here even if I am a guest. What better way to work on Rene's good graces then show him every hospitality in a very elegant home in the nation's capital? To catch the daughter, work on the father." She smiled. "Your father was a very savvy businessman to buy this house when Roosevelt asked him to come to D.C. as a 'dollar-a-year-man.' Everyone who bought in this, what was then a run-down area, came out very well. T'would make a very good impression on Rene." She looked around the spacious living room with the polished wood antiques, carved crown molding and thick oriental rugs. The windows opened all the way to the floor to allow people to walk out to the deep front porch in warm weather. Old silver gleamed in the late afternoon light, a peaceful room that bespoke wealth.

"But don't you see, that's just it, this is Dad's house not mine? Seems like I'm always staying in Dad's houses. Maybe I should get one of my own!" John started to pace the floor.

"Well-placed family is more important to the old aristocratic French then owning your own home, but Lord knows you could afford one." Chloe turned as a very sweet, motherly woman came to the living room door.

With a loving expression the newcomer spoke softly, "Mr. John, would you and Mrs. Manning like tea served in here by the fire?" Mrs. Adams had supervised the Davis house for more years then she cared to remember and the most pleasant of her duties was checking on Mr. John, as she referred to him, when she gossiped with the cook.

"None for me, Mrs. Adams. I'm going out, quite unwillingly, I might add. But how about you Chloe, tea where it's nice and warm?" John scowled.

"Why that would be lovely. Thank..." The doorbell interrupted Chloe.

"That'll be Dudley, Mrs. Adams. Tell him I'm coming." John scooped up his jacket and as he headed for the hallway he stooped to kiss Chloe on the cheek. "Would you like Mrs. Adams to bring you a shawl?" He ducked as she threw a sofa pillow at him, and then stuck his head back around the doorway. "You know I like the idea of asking Gabriel and Rene to stay here. I'll get a note off this evening or better yet an email," and he was gone.

Dudley was waiting in the hall. "Hi, John. It's not raining, only a mist. No need for a raincoat."

John said, "Dudley, you old fiend. Why are you dragging me out on a chilly night?" John started to rail, but the look on Dudley's face made him change his mind and his tone. They had known each other since childhood. From his expression, Dudley Curtis was definitely in trouble. "Glad you came by, actually. Think I rather fancy a spot of something a little stronger than tea, all right."

Once on the street, John turned to him, "What's all this about walking? My car is just around the corner. I say, do you have a personal problem, Dud? Is that what this is all about? I was never one to beat around the bush you know, if you're in trouble, just spill it out to ole' Uncle John! I have liquor at home. We could have stayed there."

Dudley looked at him horror stricken, "Good God, no. What do you mean, personal? I don't have time for anything personal. Haven't for a good while now. The reason I wanted to talk to you this afternoon is that I've just become very worried about that meeting tomorrow. You know the one Mozley set up, or perhaps you don't know what it's about. In a nutshell, the government is trying to get rid of its chemical weapons. Very tricky business. Scientifically, the best thing to do is one hell of a big bonfire, but the environmentalists are raising a stink. Since we've signed this agreement at the Chemical Weapons Convention in '97 the old forms of disposal are questionable, so we're going to neutralize some of the stockpiled weapons. They'll explain how and all about it tomorrow. The reason they've contacted you all is that some of the chemical weapons are missing or rather may be. The serial numbers seem to be mixed up."

John stopped in his tracks, "What! What are you saying?"

"We got a list of weapons from the military arsenals where they are guarded like you wouldn't believe. Those chemical weapon arsenals have the only soldiers in the U. S. with permanent shoot-to-kill authority. The brass is worried about the inconsistency of the serial numbers of the ton containers of the chemical weapons. I'm worried about something else.

"You know I have this phobia to make lists. Well I copied all the lists of the government's chemical weapons when we first got those lists from the various arsenal locations. Now, when I looked this afternoon at the lists, I wanted to get things ready for the meeting, just checking to see if those numbers are mixed up, too, well, the present lists had been changed from the ones I copied, the lists that were first reported. I always compare the old or first lists and new lists. Are you following me?" John nodded and Dudley bit his lip.

"Oh, come on now, Dud, it's really easy to misread lists of numbers, especially if you've been working 24/7." John slowed his pace.

"John, I know those lists like I know my telephone number. I counted up numbers very carefully. You see the lists from the active military arsenals have been duplicated so many times no one would try to change them. At least I didn't think so. I'm concerned about two lists: the first list that has the numbers on the ton-containers mixed-up, that's the one they're having the meeting about tomorrow, and the second list that keeps track of weapons in stockpile bases. The ton containers may have been moved or stored wrongly, but the numbers of containers seemed to add up and the serial numbers were all accounted for. At least I believed that simple explanation until today. Now I think that everything needs to be reviewed. However back to my second list, some old installations where documents are not too well kept, those are the ones that I think have been changed just recently. No large amounts mind you, just one or two weapons here and there are missing when I compared the present lists to the first lists I copied.

"Another reason I know the present lists are false is that when I was reading the lists day before yesterday to compare with the lists I'd made previously, I had spilled coffee on several of them and wiped it away. There was no mark on the lists I saw today.

"John, we're talking lethal stuff involved here. They use Sarin, VX, mustard agents such as H, HD, HT or Lewisite in these weapons. Why a tiny amount, just ten milligrams of VX on your skin could kill you in less then fifteen minutes. When you think an aspirin is 325 milligrams, you see how potent it is. Remember that guy in Bulgaria who was done in that way with VX? Just a drop on his arm!"

He stopped and looked at John. "The thing about the false lists is that they were coded and dated correctly and came through military channels with the correct date. Someone had to really know the system to be able to do that. This is an inside job. That's why I asked you to walk instead of drive. To give me time to brief you before you meet this friend of mine, Dr. Patterson. I guess the other reason I wanted to walk was because I need the exercise, haven't been out all day." Dudley covered his mouth as he coughed violently, then continued, "Patterson's waiting for us at the pub. He's an expert on the biological reactions to VX and other nerve agents. He can answer your questions about the effects of most chemical weapons. I couldn't bring it up tomorrow when everyone is there. Who knows what tracking devices are involved. These people, whoever they are, are really good."

John asked quietly, "Who's going to be at the meeting tomorrow?"

"There is Don Mozley on loan from State to Homeland Security, Andrews who's a congressional representative on the Homeland Security Committee and Armad Beel from Homeland Security, a major from the army, I don't know his name but I've seen him, Jack Bancroft from the CIA and Jo Ferguson from the FBI, you, Chloe and Richard. Until today I would have said the big shots were all above doubt and maybe they are. I just want you to tell your people in the Noir that I have these doubts."

They walked on, squashing the wet leaves underfoot. After a period of silence, John asked, through tight lips. "How many of what weapons are missing?"

"From the initial lists, one M23 land mine, two 4.2-inch M2 mortars and four M55 rockets. That's assuming the first lists were correct. We're talking really sloppy file keeping. Those rockets are the most dangerous. They have a thin aluminum shell. Some leak. Large amounts of propellants and explosives can become unstable with age. Although any chemical weapon is dangerous, to both the persons on the sending or receiving end." Dudley took out his handkerchief and blew his nose. He could feel a cold coming on. "Another thing that doesn't add up, why so few weapons? I mean most of the terrorists like to make a really big killing, not several hundred people or up to a thousand even. Of course these weapons in a heavy population area could kill a good many. Still, I think something else is going on. I've got a funny feeling there is a connection between the fact that some weapons are missing and at the same time the weapon numbers are mixed up."

"Okay, I'll alert Richard and Chloe before tomorrow. Can we call you in the morning before the meeting if they have questions?" They had reached the tavern and John reached out to hold the door.

"Sure, I'll be home until 8:30." Dudley stepped back to allow a group of diners to exit. As he did so, a man in a trench coat with the collar pulled up and hat pulled down came up behind them and bumped against Dudley and jabbed him in the neck with the point of his closed umbrella. Dudley looked startled at first as though he recognized the man, then he started to cough and grabbed for his throat to get his breath. Stumbling he fell to the ground. The scurry of people coming and going created a problem milling around the prone figure of Dudley.

A few minutes passed while John tried to get to Dudley. "Here, let me help you up. Bumbling ox, look where you're going and watch that stupid umbrella." John turned and shook his fist at the departing trench coat scurrying across the street. He nudged a partygoer aside and bent down to give his friend a hand, but Dudley's grasp was limp.

John bent closer and in the dim light saw that Dudley's eyes were beginning to glaze. Dudley tried to pull himself up. His breath was coming hard. He pulled John's face close to his lips. Dudley was gasping. His pupils were pinpoints. "The umbrella ....it was the umbrella, John. It looked like that arm ....," he started to cough again.

John propped Dudley against the stair rail and ran into the dining room, "Is there a doctor here? There's been an accident outside. Will someone call 911?" He started to run back outside.

A waiter quickly motioned to a heavyset man seated at a table near the door. "This man made a reservation for a Dr. Patterson. I'll call 911," the waiter exclaimed.

When John approached the table, the man shook his head, "Young man, I'm not a 'medical doctor'..." he began.

"Please, just come! I need help!"

After a moment's hesitation, the man slid his chair back and motioned to the John, "I'll do what I can."

"Thank God," John whispered hoarsely. "Quickly, he's outside by the door." They pushed their way through the crowd gathered around Dudley.

Patterson bent over to examine him and stiffened with recognition. "My God, it's Dudley! He's sweating profusely and his muscles are convulsing and when I felt his pulse, it's very weak." Just then, Dudley started to retch. "Here, let's see if we can get him to sit up. Otherwise he'll strangle on his vomit." For several minutes they tried to prop Dudley up, but his muscle convulsions were getting worse.

An ambulance with siren screaming pulled up beside them "Thank God you got here so quickly. My friend has collapsed. Do you have oxygen…?"

The paramedics pushed John aside as they knelt beside Dudley. The youngest, a blond-haired fellow, bent over Dudley, felt his pulse and looked at his partner. "My God, he's dead," he whispered. A woman standing within earshot started to scream.

CHAPTER TWO

"Oh, Richard, it's lovely!" Harriet exclaimed as the car rounded the last curve of the driveway and approached the house. They stopped in front of a large, three-story, brick colonial edifice perched on a hill overlooking the Potomac River.

"I was hoping to show you the house on a bright sunny spring day when the rhododendron and azaleas were in bloom, not an overcast, misty fall day." Richard leaned across her and covered her hand with his.

"I've always liked misty days. Makes you feel so romantic. Anyway, if it gets better with sun and spring, then fine. I couldn't stand to see it any grander than it is right now. Do I get a tour?" Harriet smiled up at him.

"Number one tour guide at your service." Richard jumped out and reached her side of the car in time to see Harriet, already out, close the door. No matter how he tried, she always managed to assert her independence. *No opening doors for this woman*, he thought. "Watch the stone stairs, the rain has made them slippery." The heavy oak door swung out easily as he put key to the square brass lock. "Welcome to my humble abode."

Harriet found herself in a long hallway with a living room to the right and dining room to the left. At the other end of the hallway was a door presumably opening to the outside. A curved stair railing began at the corner of the dining room door and wound its way up toward a second story. If she craned her neck, she could see the stairway winding on up to what must be a third story. The stair treads were made of a cherry wood generally reserved for fine furniture veneer.

"The Coopers live here and take care of the place for me when I'm gone. Sarah and Jim Cooper are an older couple, have been with the family forty years. They are in Dansville right now visiting a new grandson. I asked them to leave us some food and lay a fire. Do you want to see the house first or have a little sherry and a fire?"

"Oh, a fire and sherry! I need to get my breath and enjoy this elegance. I'm really overwhelmed." Harriet pulled her sweater closer around her body and shivered.

"Fine! Come here and sit by the fireplace. I know you have to get to work early tomorrow, and this is a long way to go for dinner, but I couldn't wait any longer. So we're going to crowd a lot into this evening. Beside introducing you to my house, we have some serious discussing to do." Richard talked as he strode over to the fireplace and busied around checking the flue and stuffing the newspapers closer under the kindling, Harriet surveyed the room. A deep Kashan oriental rug covered the floor, leather and damask wing chairs and polished wooden Windsor chairs were placed facing the fireplace. A blue damask camel-back sofa was on the other side. Long windows with wooden shutters faced the porch on the front and a patio to the rear. Over the mantel was an oil portrait of a dignified white-haired gentleman in a frock coat. Richard struck a match and the dry kindling immediately began to crackle. He glanced up and saw her appraising the portrait.

"He's my grandfather. I was named for him. My Dad was a swash-buckling, carefree type right up through college, or so I hear. Gramps loved him and indulged his every whim. Dad enlisted in World War II. I've got pictures of him in his uniform, a real heartthrob, fighter pilot! He spent a good deal of time in France. This really upset Gramps. Bull-dog English, he had a dim view of the French. I don't know what happened overseas, but when Dad came back, the

Coopers said he was different. He seemed sad, distracted and very serious. He entered the bank with Gramps and married my mother, a true southern belle. She worshiped my dad but he somehow seemed remote both to her and to me." Richard sat still and looked into the fire.

Harriet waited, silently. "You know, you are a very good listener." He grinned. "How about some sherry now?" Richard walked to the buffet against the wall facing the fireplace and poured two glasses from the Waterford crystal carafe. He came to her, handed her a glass and sat on the footstool at her feet. "I brought you here to ask you a question, but first I must tell you something that may affect your answer, so bear with me. When I was just out of grad school, I joined this organization. I'm still a member and I would like to remain as a member, but there is a certain amount of danger involved. Really I guess I shouldn't go any further." He looked away. "You see I wanted to ask you to marry me, but if I continue the work I do, work that I feel is meaningful, well, I don't want to sound dramatic but some risk is involved. I love you, Harriet. Could you accept me and let me continue in my work? I guess the thing that really bothers me is, will you be safe if you are married to me? I'm saying this very badly."

"Yes, you are saying it badly. My, aren't we being vague? Don't you trust me enough to tell me more about this 'secret organization'?" She looked him full in the eyes. Her manner had cooled.

Richard stood and went to the fire. He took a poker from the rack by the fireplace and poked the fire, then turned to her. "I can honestly say I trust you more than anyone I've ever known. So I am going to tell you all about my involvement. I have never spoken of this to anyone who is not associated with it. But I must request your silence, whether you marry me or not. Many lives are involved." He came back and took a seat on the footstool at her feet, but he turned away and stared into the fire. As he gazed at the fire, it seemed to grow brighter and mesmerize him. It seemed to symbolize the danger and excitement that had always fascinated him. "When I was a child, one of our neighbors filled my head with the stories of Nazi atrocities and the tales of the French heroes of the underground. My father never spoke of his experiences, and he winced whenever the

Nazis or France were mentioned in connection with the war. So the exaggerated stories I heard were from this neighbor, who was 4-F and glamorized everything.

"When I went to Europe after grad school, my friends told me about a secret organization, La Fleur Noir that gave protection for the downtrodden. They had roused my dreams and imagination. I joined the secret brotherhood. I never told my father and Gramps would have killed me if he ever found out. He hated the French. Sometimes, at night, the faces of associates of the Noir flood back over me and I have nightmares. I have never told anyone that little item before, either." He shuddered.

Harriet put her hand to his shoulder and said softly, "Tell me about the Noir."

In a distant, trance like tone he began, "After the French Revolution, Jacques and Antoine Begue, friends of Lafayette, formed La Fleur Noir, a resistance group supported by French noblemen. The purpose was to protect their friends from the injustices of the fanatics that took over the government. They took the king's emblem, La Fleur-de-Lis, and colored it black for the group's shadowy existence. As the years passed, the organization was passed on to the founder's sons and daughters and their friends. They continued to work as vigilantes for the oppressed.

"During the World Wars it was a significant part of the resistance movement. The Noir, as the members called it, continues now to help those in need of help anywhere in the world. Always a member suggests where help is needed. We got a call yesterday to a meeting in Washington with some military types. I'm afraid a very dangerous mission is shaping up. I feel like a fool telling you all this and then asking you to marry me. I just don't want you to go into marriage blind to the possible effects of my commitment. I almost didn't ask you, but the thought of not having you with me every possible moment has become unbearable." He turned and faced her.

"Richard, you are like a little boy. Please tell me the rest. There is more isn't there? What happened at The Noir? You've gone this far, tell me all the story." Harriet drew her hand across his shoulder.

Richard stood and looked down at her. "Can you see into all your patients like this, Doctor?" He poked the fire viciously and started to pace up and down the floor again. "While I was on a mission, I met this French girl who was also in the Noir. She was married. I'm not proud of what I did. We both tried to keep away from each other, but we were young and daring and very much in love, or thought we were. She got pregnant and couldn't bear to tell her husband. I think she loved us both. Do you think that is possible?" He stopped his pacing and looked back at her and then away. "She went back to her husband and gave birth to our daughter. She stayed away until the little girl was about three years old. Then she came back to the Noir to do one last mission. She said she couldn't help herself."

He went to the sideboard and poured himself more sherry, lifted the carafe and looked at Harriet inquiringly. She shook her head. He continued pacing. "Well, it seems she came back with the intent to end her torment. She exposed herself needlessly and was killed. I tried to drag her to safety but it was too late." He stopped and stared out the window at the rain. After a few moments he continued talking to the rain-patterned window. "I had to go and tell her husband. We cried on each other's shoulders. I felt so guilty. I never thought I could ever love anyone like that again until I met you this spring." He turned and faced her.

Harriet rose and went to him. She reached up and put his head on her shoulder. "Yes," she said, "I will marry you. I'm glad you told me all of it. I don't want us to have any secrets. I love you too, Richard."

He just held her close for a long time. The fire burned slowly down. Still holding her close, he sat back on the sofa and whispered into her hair, "When can we set the date? I don't want to wait, Harriet. Life is too short, too uncertain to wait."

"Well, I haven't thought about this, but off the top of my head I think we should get married here in this town at the darling little country church we passed on the way up and have all our friends afterwards to this house, your home, which will be our home. I want my folks to come from Iowa and I want to wear a lovely dress and carry lilies."

Richard laughed, "For just talking off the top of your head, I'm impressed. Do you always plan so quickly? Does practicing medicine make you so decisive? Sounds good to me. When?"

"Next week! No matter what a woman says, at one time or another, she has thought 'what will my wedding be like'? So it's never really ever off the top of her head." He laughed deliciously and hugged her. The warm intimate moment was broken when the phone rang.

"This has to be a mistake. No one knows I'm here." Richard unfolded his left arm that had gone stiff and stood up. He reached for the phone on the table as he grinned at Harriet. "Hello. Chloe, how did you know I was here? What's happened? Oh no! How? When? Have you contacted John?" He paused with a worried frown. "Have you called anyone else? Why not? Have you called Don Mozley? Dudley set up that meeting with him tomorrow. Why not?" He paused for several minutes listening intently. "Oh, I see. Yes, we'll come back. We should be there in about forty-five minutes." He hung up the phone and frowned.

"Well, it looks like the lovely evening I'd planned is gone up in smoke. That was Chloe. Remember you met her when you went with us to the Smithwick Labs and we were able to stop the illegal use of smallpox virus? It seems a friend of John's, Dudley Curtis, was murdered. Or at least has died mysteriously. I'm going to have to go back to Washington. Looks like my job is already getting in our way. Will you forgive me?" Richard sat beside her and looked steadily into her eyes.

"Darling, you're talking to a doctor. Our lives are always put on hold." She laughed lightly and got up. "It's a good thing we didn't plan to spend the weekend!"

"No, it's not! That would have been wonderful, just the thought makes me happy. But I must content myself with the fact that you said 'yes' and not ask for more. At least not right now! Look, Sarah Cooper must have put our dinner in the fridge. Could you bundle it up while I make some phone calls?"

"Not even married and already I'm to do the meals!" Harriet laughed as she went in search of the kitchen, which she found behind the dining room, a lovely white kitchen. On the top shelf of the refrigerator was a plate of fried chicken and beside it a dish of potato salad and a tray of fresh veggies. *Well, Sarah Cooper, I'm really going to get along just fine with you,* Harriet thought. *I like a well-organized woman who plans for all possibilities*. She opened drawers until she found the wrapping papers and sacks and was busily engaged when Richard came up behind her.

He put his arm around her waist, and hugged her to him. "You look right at home here." He laughed.

"Let's get this straight, one of my conditions is that we share the house work. Okay?" She grinned up in his face. "What do you do with the fireplace?"

"Oops, I forgot. Not like me. Must have my mind on other things. Package that up and we'll be off. I'll just bank the fire and meet you in the hall."

The rain had begun in earnest as they dashed for the car. "Well, that was certainly a short visit. Here's hoping your next will be longer. On the other hand, what more could I ask? You said yes. It will be all right and I'll do all in my power to keep you out of the Noir dealings. I promise. I will keep you out of it!" He hesitated with his hand on the wheel.

Harriet pretended not to hear as she busied herself unwrapping some food. She knew the world too well to believe that was possible, but she smiled up at him, "Do I get to see the rest of the house next time? The bedrooms? Is there a basement? A dungeon? Do you want me to hand you some food as you drive?"

"Yes, to all the above, except we don't have a dungeon. Start with that drumstick. I'm famished." He turned the key, and the car lurched on the wet pavement as he headed back down the long driveway.

"Tell me about Dudley Curtis. Who is he and why would someone want to kill him? What has that to do with you?" Harriet handed him the meat and tucked a paper napkin over his leg.

"Dudley and John grew up together, neighbors. Their fathers were friends, served in the army together. Dudley was always the more serious one. When John attended the university, Dudley went to West Point. He's been in or somehow attached to the military ever since, mostly doing intelligence work I think. He's the one who contacted us about a meeting tomorrow. I haven't had time to fill John in on it and I'm not sure I should be talking to you about it. I have no idea why anyone would want to murder him, if it is murder." He looked worried.

"Well since we're not to have any secrets from now on, you'd better talk to me about the meeting." She handed him a carrot stick and took a piece of chicken for herself.

"The army has asked The Noir to do a check on the locations and serial numbers of their chemical weapons. Seems there is some confusion accounting for the weapons' placement. They need an outside check and naturally don't want to ask another military service or another government to do it. So the Noir, the FBI and CIA are all hooked up with Homeland Security. Nothing to be concerned about, just a routine check, or at least so it seemed. From what I can gather there are two problems here. The first is that while all the weapons are accounted for number-wise, according to the serial numbers, they are in the wrong places!"

Harriet started to laugh. "I know this could be dangerous, but you must admit, it's funny. How could you possibly misplace a chemical weapon?"

"Well, until Dudley's death, I thought it was just sloppy paper work. Perhaps the army should get the UPS to do their tracking for them! Now, I'm not so sure it's that simple."

With her mouth full, Harriet asked, "So what's the second problem?"

"The next problem is the military's, not mine, and that's how to dispose of the chemical weapons once they're sure they have them all. You see when the army put out the contracts for these weapons the specifications just said how to make them and no mention was made of how to disassemble them. We've not made any weapons since the '60's and we have some from World War I. So there is probably some leakage. Now that we've ratified the Chemical Weapons Convention in April 1997, we're committed to get rid of all these weapons as well as the chemicals by 2007. Of course nobody thinks we can. All the signers will probably request an extension." Richard frowned both at his statement and the increasing pounding of the rain. "With this cloud burst we'll be lucky to get to John's in three hours!"

Harriet became very quiet. In a subdued voice she asked, "What chemicals are you talking about?"

"Well there are several groups of chemicals called poison gases, really they are mostly liquids. There are blistering agents like mustard, then also choking agents, blood agents, harassing agents, psychological agents, binary agents and nerve agents. The last bothers me the most, especially VX. I don't know why I'm explaining chemical weapons to you. You probably know more about them then I do or at least their biological effects." Richard took out his handkerchief and wiped the inside of the window next to him that was clouding up.

Harriet drew in her breath sharply. "Lordy, yes, I know of VX and some of the others! You're right; I'm familiar with their biological effects. How much of these weapons does everyone have?"

"According to the national stockpiles declared by the Chemical Weapons Convention signers, the U.S. has about 63,000,000 pounds of chemical agents, Russia about 80,000,000. I don't know about India and South Korea. China and Iran haven't declared theirs. Some countries didn't sign like Israel, Libya, and North Korea. At the end of the Gulf War, Iraq had 40,000pounds." Richard glanced over at her. "What I'm telling you is common knowledge, no secrets."

"Why, Richard, you're talking about enough destructive power to kill huge numbers of men, women, children and animals several times over!" She looked at him horrified.

"Yes, I know. We all remember the awful effect of mustard agent in World War I. But few of us know that the Japanese used chemical agents in Manchuria in 1930's, the same decade that the Italians used mustard agent in Ethiopia. In 1963 the Egyptians used mustard agent against the Yemenis in the Arabian Peninsula. The Russians used chemical agents in Afghanistan. In the 1980's and 90's when Iraq was afraid it would lose the war with Iran, it used mustard agent against Iran and hydrogen cyanide gas in 1988 against the Kurds. They may have used VX also. Remember the Sarin attack in the Tokyo subway by the Shrinrikyo cult? It goes on and on.

"Did you know the Germans had mustard weapons but never used them during World War II? Several reasons are given why they didn't: Hitler was gassed in World War I and was personally opposed to it as were Allied generals who had faced mustard in WWI as junior officers. Another reason, and I feel the real reason, was that the Germans thought the Allies had nerve agents since the Allies had been doing research on insecticides which by the way are what most nerve agents were derived from. I guess you could call nerve agents 'the bugs revenge'! Actually, the Allies had not discovered nerve agents during World War II.

"But everyone in World War II had gas masks just in case they were needed. Walt Disney even designed a gas mask for American children. It looked like Mickey Mouse. The U.S. and Britain were prepared to use mustard to retaliate defensively if they were gassed. Ironically the only mustard casualties in World War II were the American and British troops themselves. The Nazis bombed the *SS John Harvey* in the harbor at Bari, Italy and the fire and explosions loosed the mustard bombs on the ship in huge clouds over the ships in the harbor and the city. No one knows how many civilians were killed but about 600 service men were.

"Of all of the chemical weapons, VX scares me the most. For example, after an attack with most of the chemical agents, the enemy is dead or inactive and troops can enter an area, but with VX, nobody can enter safely for weeks or months...it's a no man's land. VX remains active for weeks or months on the ground and equipment. You're a doctor, how do the chemical agents work?" Richard rubbed his handkerchief over the side window again.

Harriet wrapped her chicken in a napkin and put it back in the paper bag. "My work in the Center for Disease Control has been with bacteria or viruses, but we were briefed several times on the chemicals used in warfare. Mostly they talked about either blistering agents or nerve agents. All the effects depend on how much is administered and where on the body and what kind of health the person has. There are lots of other variables such as temperature and humidity.

"Nerve agents are members of a group of chemicals called organophosphates. In the body, acetylcholine acts on both the central and peripheral nervous systems to stimulate muscular action. Normally an enzyme, acetyl cholinesterase or AChE stops the action of acetylcholine stimulating the muscles. But nerve agents bind to the AChE and make it inactive. So the acetylcholine keeps on acting and stimulating the muscles. You get neuromuscular effects like twitching, respiratory failure or paralysis, or autonomic nervous system effects like small pupil size in the eye or loss of fluid such as drooling, sweating and vomiting. Then there are the central nervous effects. Mild effects are slurred speech, depression or confusion. The more drastic effects are convulsions, coma and death.

"The nerve agents enter through the lungs or through the skin. Once again the effect depends on the amount used. The first treatment is an antidote, then to wash all areas, put the clothes in a plastic bag and burn them. Two drugs are used as an antidote: atropine and pralidoxine. The former blocks the acetylcholine receptor, the latter blocks the binding of the agent to AChE. All our troops, and as a matter of fact anyone working with these agents or in their vicinity get three kits called Mark I containing these two drugs and autoinjectors. Medical care persons must also protect themselves from contamination while maintaining ventilation and correcting cardiovascular abnormalities. This can be dangerous work as exemplified by the caregivers in the Iraq-Iran War in the '80s who became exposed themselves. Now aren't you sorry you asked?" She smiled at him and offered another piece of chicken.

"No more chicken. I think I lost my appetite." Richard wiped the window glass again. The moisture was dripping down the inside of the car door.

"What did Chloe have to say about Dudley's death? How did it happen? Had she told John?" Harriet started to gnaw nervously on a carrot stick, her only sign of lack of composure.

"Chloe said John was with Dudley when it happened. Seems Dudley was stabbed with an umbrella as they were entering a bar in Georgetown. Dudley had planned to meet a Dr. Patterson at the bar. This doctor recognized some of the symptoms of poisoning when Dudley collapsed and that's why they're calling it murder. What I don't understand is why Chloe said they hadn't called Mozley." Richard frowned at the rain on the window. "Dudley's always worked closely with Mozley, but John was adamant about talking with me before he called Mozley. I'm afraid it's tied up with this chemical warfare meeting we're suppose to attend tomorrow. Blast!

Dudley was a really decent sort. I didn't know him as well as John did. He's pretty broken up according to Chloe."

"Where is Chloe staying in Washington?" Harriet tried to calm herself by putting the remains of dinner back in the paper bag. She could tell Richard's thoughts were elsewhere.

"She's bunking at John's house or rather his father's house. The Davises must own a house in practically every town in the world. Take banking money, triple it, add it to old family money of his wife then have the whole lot managed by a very adroit businessman, John's father, and the amount is unimaginable!" He laughed a mirthless laugh. He was silent for a moment then continued. "Since this lovely evening seems to be disintegrating, I want to tell you something else." He paused so long Harriet thought he had forgotten what he wanted to say. She waited patiently.

"Well, the fact is," he cleared his throat, "the fact is, the daughter I told you about, remember the love child of the French girl? She's Chloe's granddaughter. Marie, her mother was the French girl I've been talking about. Well, my daughter and her father are coming to the U.S. next week and I've asked them to come out and stay with me ...that is us…on the Potomac. Her name is Gabriel." He stopped talking at a total loss for words.

Harriet prompted him, "And…"

"Well, it seems she has some kind of childish crush on me." Here, he stopped and Harriet could see he was coloring.

"What? You're telling me some sweet young French thing will be here in time for our wedding and by the way she's your daughter, doesn't know it, and is in love with you?" Harriet pressed her feet against the floorboard as there was nothing else to push. Then she started to laugh. "Well, this will certainly be a night to remember…a proposal, a murder and now another woman! Do you have any other little goodies to share before you take me home?"

"Look, I've really screwed this up I know. I mean I had it all planned out so well. A pleasant evening, a calm discussion. Please just bear with me. You'll like Gabriel and she'll like you. How could she help it?" He reached for her hand. They were approaching the Davis house in Georgetown.

Harriet stared at him unbelievingly. *No one could be that naive, truly*, she thought. *Did he really believe they would all be palsy-chums? What about the French father, where would he fit in all this?* She raised her eyes to the road and shouted, "Watch out!"

An Army jeep swerved in front of them just as they were approaching the Davis house. "Damn!" Richard pulled the car to a vacant parking spot just in time to avoid a head on collision. They both sat still for a few minutes and caught their breath.

"That driver was looking back at the house and not where he was going. Did you see the man? Did you recognize him?" Harriet tried to keep her voice even.

"I didn't even look, I was to busy trying to get out of his way. Stupid dummy! Probably drunk! Lord, what else can happen tonight?' He turned off the motor and silently opened the car door.

CHAPTER THREE

A silence seemed to have settled over the Davis house, yard and surrounding area, the silence of a death in the family. Even the falling rain sounded subdued. Richard raised the heavy brass knocker several times; the resulting dull thudding echoed down the street. A very sweet-faced, middle-aged woman with eyes red from weeping answered the knock. "Oh, Dr. Moore! Thank heavens you're here. Isn't this terrible? Mr. John is just beside himself and poor Mr. Dudley; just tonight he was at the door, so cheerful. But what am I doing keeping you standing here at the door. Come in, come in." She looked enquiringly at Harriet.

"We came as soon as we heard, Mrs. Adams. Yes, this is terrible." He put his arm around Harriet's shoulders. "Mrs. Adams, this is Dr. Hobbs. Where are Chloe and John?"

Mrs. Adams noted the arm over the shoulders and smiled through her tears, then she returned to her sadness. "Mrs. Manning is in the living room. Mr. John has locked himself in the library. Maybe you could talk to him. Would you like some tea?" As she talked, she led them down the hall. They saw Chloe sitting in a wing chair, staring into the fireplace. She looked up as they approached her.

"Richard, thank heaven you're here. Please go and talk to John. I'm afraid this, on top of the other deaths he's witnessed this past year is really creating a serious problem." She stopped when she spotted Harriet and Richard unconsciously put his arm over Harriet's shoulders again in a protecting motion then removed it as quickly. Nothing was ever lost on Chloe. She walked over and took both of Harriet's hands in hers and said, "Thank you for coming, Dr. Hobbs." She glanced at Richard and continued, "You're becoming one of the family, always being there when a crisis develops. First, when we cornered the killers at the Smithwick Labs and now this."

"How kind of you to remember me. What can we do?" Harriet asked.

"Richard, if you could talk to John, please. He's having a dreadful time of it. Perhaps you could keep me company here, Dr. Hobbs." She looked over her shoulder at Mrs. Adams. "Could you bring some fresh tea, Mrs. Adams? This looks like a long night." Mrs. Adams nodded, sniffling, not trusting her voice, and scurried from the room.

"I'll be back in a few minutes." Richard squeezed Harriet's hand and followed Mrs. Adams into the hall.

"Do sit down, my Dear." Chloe motioned to the wing chair opposite hers and seated herself again. "I believe Richard has come to depend on you a great deal. And may I add, he seems to care for you immensely." She leaned back and waited.

Harriet was never one to act coy. She looked directly at Chloe. "Yes, he asked me to marry him tonight and I said yes."

"Thank heaven! I am so glad, for both of you. He's an intelligent, caring man and will make you very happy." Chloe leaned across the small space separating them and squeezed Harriet's hand.

Surprised, Harriet exclaimed, "You're not upset? Richard told me about Marie and Gabriel. And I feel I am not betraying him by saying he also told me of his involvement in the Noir."

Chloe looked away into the fire. "No, I'm not upset. Richard and I share a feeling of guilt about Marie. He feels he caused her death and I feel I might have been able to prevent it. That is all over. If we keep regretting the past there is no room for the present or future. I hope you will be very happy and I will do all I can to assist you with Gabriel. Richard probably told you of her crush on him. He's quite upset with it all. I must admit that could be a problem. She's sophisticated and mature beyond her years, and very determined! A big help is that John is very much in love with her, perhaps more than even he knows. We'll work on that together, shall we?"

Mrs. Adams, bringing in a tea tray, forestalled any further talk. A few minutes later John stumbled into the room followed by Richard. He seated himself on the sofa with a nod to Harriet and Chloe. Richard waited until Mrs. Adams had left the room and said, "I've been talking to John here. It seems Dr. Patterson, whom they were to meet at Hanson's Bar, is not a medical doctor but a professor of physiology at John Hopkins. Dudley had contacted him to find out more about the effects of chemicals used in warfare. Since, Dr. Patterson was there immediately after Dudley's attack, he has volunteered to work with the coroner to do an autopsy and check the tissue sample for chemicals. The results should be in early in the morning. It seems Dudley was concerned about some missing chemical weapons and was convinced that the cover up was an inside job. So he was hesitant about mentioning his suspicions to the group at the meeting tomorrow morning." Richard paused for breath.

John leaned forward with his head in his hands murmuring, "I can't believe it happened and so damn fast! If only I had insisted that we drive, or talk here!"

"Which brings up the subject of the meeting tomorrow. Do we bring up the topic of Dudley's doubts before everyone or just one or two?" Richard started pacing the floor.

A flash of interest crossed John's face as puzzles always challenged him. He straightened up and asked, "We both know Mozley and have worked with him on several cases. Perhaps if we only tell one person, then if there is a leak we can be sure who it is? Please, God, don't let the monster be Mozley!"

Richard stopped his pacing. "I think you're right. We have to get into Dudley's office and check his lists. Mozley could make that possible."

"The last thing Dudley whispered before he went into that terrible coughing was 'it looked like that arm…'. God, if I only knew what he was trying to say!"

Chloe went to the sofa and sat beside him. "You did what Dudley asked. You followed his advice and went with him. Perhaps Dudley suspected the danger and wanted you there beside him. Certainly that is what friends are for, to back you up. The fact that he asked you is the greatest gesture of trust. Don't question his choice."

John lifted his head. "Do you always know the right thing to say?" For the first time since he entered the room, he straightened his shoulders.

"Not always," sighed Chloe, "I didn't say the right thing to Marie the night before she died." She glanced at Richard and he winced. Then she continued, "Which brings up a new topic. Richard, Harriet told me you have proposed and she's accepted. I am so very glad. How strange, always in the midst of sorrow and fear, something good surfaces. Enough to give you hope. I wish you both all the happiness in the world"

It took a moment for John to grasp what she had just said. "Lord, I don't know what to say! I'm dazed. I'm torn between grief and guilt for Dudley and relief and genuine happiness for you and Richard. Harriet, I am truly pleased for you both. I can honestly say Richard is worthy of you, Harriet. You've done yourself proud, old man." Then he gasped as another thought struck him, "But who the hell is going to tell Gabriel?"

John sat gazing out the window at Nebraska Avenue Center, the location of the Department of Homeland Security. The rain was still pelting the window with a heavy bombardment. *Lord, will the rain ever stop,* he thought. *Maybe the skies are crying for Dudley.* He tried to shake the morbid thought and concentrate. Eight people were seated around a large mahogany table, their folders and papers spread before them. The meeting room was cool, heat not yet turned on in the building. The walls were government standard cream-colored, the chairs regulation swivel back and uncomfortable.

Don Mozley began in a somber tone, unusual for him, "Arnold Andrews cannot be with us today. A situation has developed involving a possible terrorist attack, and he has a congressional committee meeting. I'll fill him in on what we discuss here. In the meantime,

Beel here will be carrying on for DHS." Don hesitated, "Last night a dear friend, Dudley Curtis died. His death is still under investigation. He was supposed to be here with us today." He paused. John looked up and down the table to see the effects of the announcement.

Jo Ferguson uttered a little cry, just a yelp and lowered her head and clutched her hands together. Apparently the FBI hadn't given out the news yet to its people. John wondered if she had had a closer then just work attachment to Dudley.

Jack Bancroft nodded. He reached over to put a hand on Jo's arm and she brushed him away. The CIA must have informed him. Jack had worked with Dudley on several army investigations and was considered an ally whenever Dudley needed one, which was seldom. John had seen them having lunch together many times, both in heated discussions or arguments over a case.

Both Beel and an army major seated next to him looked interested but uninvolved. Mozley continued, turning to address the major, "Dowell, I know you and Beel had never met Dudley, but if any of you have any information that you think may have bearing on this investigation, please let me know." He cleared his throat. He had known Dudley a long time and this situation was hard for him.

Don Mozley was definitely not conducting the meeting in his usual breezy style. "Gentlemen, Ladies thank you all for coming. Today we are asking your help about a minor infringement of some government procedures." *Minor infringement my ass*, thought John. *Losing track of chemical weapons! What would he call World War II, a 'regrettable incident'?*" Don continued, "We've asked you all to come and help us to get some government accounting straight. We all represent different groups that are involved in this matter. I am on loan as it were from the State Department. The army has requested our help since State provides oversight on chemical demilitarization along with Congress, DOD, EPA and several other groups. I guess State is involved in case we step on some foreign toes. As you all know there are five divisions of the Department of Homeland Security and Armad Beel here is Under Secretary of the Science and Technology Division," he nodded to the bearded man on his right. "So he'll be coordinating all your work and keep you all up-to-date on all the goings on. The U.S. Army is in charge of carrying out the actual chemical demilitarization. It seems the army has mixed up some of its records and our job is to get them straightened out. So I'll turn this meeting over to Major Dowell of the U.S. Army to explain." John thought to himself, *Don, you only used four 'you alls'. For a Georgia boy, this is a first. You are really taking this hard.*

The Major had been sitting rigidly straight all through the introduction and now rose, stiff as a ramrod as if he were going to salute the whole group. He cleared his throat. "As Don here has mentioned, we've had some problems with our accounting procedure. Every chemical weapon has a serial number and we keep track of what weapons are where. But we have gathered chemical weapons at seven places: Umatilla, Oregon; Anniston, Alabama; Pine Bluff, Arkansas; Tooele, Utah; Blue Grass, Kentucky; Pueblo, Colorado; and Johnston Atoll, Pacific Ocean. As you can see, we have a lot to keep track of, although we shouldn't count Johnston Atoll since that stockpile's been destroyed." He smiled thinking this a bit of humor to minimize the situation.

"What about your non-weaponized stockpile chemicals like chemical agents in containers that are in Aberdeen, Maryland or Newport, Indiana? That makes nine not seven military places. Or the non-stockpiled materials: binary-compounds and recovered weapons? It's the chemical containers not the weapons that you've goofed up on, isn't that correct? Or have you mismanaged both?" Jo Ferguson had obviously done her homework and was fighting to regain her composure. She was a pert, five foot brunette with a no nonsense gaze.

The Major obviously didn't like to be interrupted and he decidedly didn't like to be interrupted by a non-military and a woman at that. He cleared his throat and waved his hand as if brushing aside a nuisance mosquito. "We do have a little problem with the tracking of these containers. To continue, in accordance with the Chemical Weapons Convention, the CWC, we are preparing to destroy our chemical weapons as well as all the chemical agents. Not the rockets or mortars if they can be decontaminated after the chemical agent is removed. Actually, we've already incinerated all CW's at the Johnston Atoll. That facility has become a wildlife preserve. About 25% of the CW's at Tooele, Utah have been destroyed to date. Incinerators have been built or will be built in Anniston, Alabama; Toole, Utah; Pine Bluff, Arkansas and Umatilla, Oregon and hopefully, if public opinion can be controlled, we will incinerate those CW's. We're going to chemically neutralize the agents at Aberdeen, Maryland and Newport, Indiana followed by biotreatment of the Maryland mustard agent and aqueous oxidation followed by bio-oxidation of the Indiana Sarin, VX, etc. Neutralization is a new procedure and still under scrutiny."

Richard was doodling on the note pad in front of him. He had written down the names of all the people in the room plus the absent Arnold Andrews and each of their connections to the committee. John glanced over and stopped scanning halfway down the list and stared at the name Armad Beel as if a connection had been made to Dudley's last words. He reached over and with a pencil underlined the first three letters of Arnold Andrews and Armand Beel and looked at Richard who nodded as if he understood the reference to Dudley's last utterance. Then Richard underlined the first three letters of the word 'army' following Dowell's name. He nonchalantly tore off the sheet, crumpled it and put it in his pocket. He smiled at John and turned his attention back to Major Dowell who was again being questioned by Jo Ferguson.

"Once the material is chemically neutralized, what next? What do you do with the remains and what about the plant that does the chemical neutralizing? It's obviously contaminated, so is the plant neutralized? I take it the plant will not be confused with some other site in your record keeping." Jo was getting worked up about this.

"This is not something you have to consider at this meeting. We are here today to try and straighten out tracking methods. The chemical neutralization process is new and scientists are working out the incidentals. You don't have to do that!" Major Dowell did everything but pat her on the head and say 'not to worry, Dear'. He had underestimated Jo Ferguson.

She leaned back in her chair and twirling her pencil laughed, too loud, a laugh that could border on sneering, "How do we know, if you can't keep track of dangerous chemicals supposed to be in your control, that you can even attempt something as complicated as chemical neutralization of CW's in highly populated areas, let alone safely dispose of the remains? By the way, Fed Ex has mastered its tracking procedure. Perhaps you should take lessons from them."

Major Dowell turned very red in the face. Before he could speak, Don Mozley interrupted, "Now, let's keep an eye on why we're here. Our purpose is not to point a finger, or argue how to get rid of CW's, but to see how the serial numbers on the chemical containers or CTs got mixed up and if any CTs are missing. Any suggestions, you all?"

Richard cleared his throat, "I assume the serial numbers are all kept on a computerized list. John here is a computer expert, with access to the facilities of a long list of computer companies that he owns. Perhaps he could go over the recording program for these lists and see if there is a fluke of some kind. Also, we could visit the sites and check the storage facilities, just to ascertain that there are no irregularities in the storage arrangements."

Major Dowell started to sputter, "Sir, are you insinuating that we don't know computers in the army or that we are inept at our storage? Who are you anyway and whom do you represent?"

"Obviously the army is incapable of one or both, storage tracking or computer expertise, or we wouldn't be here, would we?" Richard answered coolly.

Once again Don Mozley intervened and addressed Major Dowell directly, "Drs. Moore and Davis and Mrs. Manning represent an agency we have used before to quietly and discreetly investigate irregularities. I expect all of you to give them your help. Your suggestion is excellent, Richard. Sounds good to me. Any objections or further suggestions?" He pointedly ignored the Major and before anyone could bring up another question, he said. "Good, let's go with it. Meeting dismissed!" Don turned with a sigh of relief to pick up his papers from the desk in front of him. *Why did he want the meeting over so quickly?* John thought. *Something to hide? Upset about Dudley?*

Major Dowell stomped from the room glowering at Jo as he left. Slowly a dejected Jo Ferguson headed for the door. "Wait up, Jo," Jack Bancroft called as he quickly picked up his papers and hurried out after her.

"If you will permit me, Dr. Davis is it? I will be happy to show you our computer programs and put you in touch with the army programmer." Armad Beel approached John with his hand out stretched.

John hesitated and then took the hand. "Thank you." He turned to Richard, "Okay if I leave you and get in touch later?"

"Fine. I'll drop by your house this afternoon." Richard waved him off and turned to Don and Chloe. "Could we just sit here and talk a minute?" Don seated himself again and both Chloe and Richard moved up to the seats opposite him. "Don, I assume this room is bug proof?"

Don looked at him surprised, "Well, I should hope so! What's going on here, Richard?

"As you know, John was with Dudley when he died. According to John, Dudley had contacted him to discuss an irregularity in the lists that he got from some older sites that stored CW's. It seems Dudley made copies of the first lists that were sent in and then compared them to some more recent lists and the two didn't jibe. Some CW's were missing. This has nothing to do with the serial number and storage problems you discussed today."

Don whistled, "What was missing from the first list?" He wrinkled his forehead and thought. "And why didn't John mention this to me earlier or bring it up at the meeting today?"

"Apparently, the last list that came in, the doctored list, came through military channels and was predated. Dudley felt someone who knew all the systems had to do that. So he didn't know whom to trust at the meeting."

Don sat up straighter. "Does that mean me, too? I've known Dudley for years. Could he have suspected me?"

Richard answered calmly, "If you were in his shoes would you suspect everybody?"

Slowly Don responded, "Yes, I guess, so. What about you? Do you suspect me?"

"Would I be telling you all this if I did?" Richard smiled.

Don turned to Chloe, "Notice he didn't say he did trust me. You are one slick operator, Richard. So if I follow you correctly, you are going to tell just me and see what happens. If there is a misstep, I'm the one! Okay. Try me. What do we do next?" Don sat back with his old grin on his face and stroked his beard.

"We need a background check on all the people who were here today. We'll do our own, naturally, but if you could give us checks, it would save a lot of time and point us in the right direction. Also, you may have something on these people that would be classified information and while we could get it, as I say, your check would be faster." Richard faced him.

"Done," said Mozley, "next."

"We need to get into Dudley's office and see if we can find these lists he talked about. Can you get us in?" Richard asked.

"Of course. We'll go now." Mozley stood up. "Come on, Chloe. I don't trust a handsome woman like you down here all by yourself with all these suspicious, sneaky characters like myself about."

He led them to the elevator and up to the third floor. At the door he stopped. "Now I know this is going to incriminate me, but I do have a key to his office. I got it this morning to get his things to send to his folks. When I called they were pretty broken up about it. Everyone who knew him is. That was one mighty fine young man. Or as my grand pappy down in Georgia would have said, 'a fine Christian gentleman'." He reached down and unlocked the door. "Lord Almighty, what's happened here!"

The room looked like a hurricane had hit it. Drawers emptied and upturned, papers strewn over the floor, chairs upset.

Richard whistled and asked, "So, who else had a key?"

"Well, Armad would. He's one of the division heads in command here and looks after all the offices and procedures. I just came over from the State Department about four months ago. And I guess the janitor and cleaning lady have one." Don shook his head.

Richard moved to the phone and unscrewed the cap from the end of the receiver. He tapped it on his hand and a small disk fell out. "Well, this explains how whoever was interested found out that Dudley was going to meet John and go to the pub. Whoever searched the office missed the bug or else forgot it or didn't know it existed. You can get them to check for fingers prints both on the bug and this room, Don." He wrapped the disc in his handkerchief and handed it to Mozley. Silently, they all viewed the papers and personal paraphernalia lying about. "Lord, where to start. Well, the stuff lying about apparently was looked at and rejected."

Chloe had seated herself at the computer. She ran her hand around the monitor. "Richard, can you lift this?" He came over and raised the heavy screen. She slid her hand under it and pulled out a folded list. "Now, if I were going to hide a computer list and I had a methodical mind like Dudley's, I'd hide it under the computer! I notice dust around all the sides of the monitor but this side. Looks like this side's been smudged." She smiled and handed the list to Richard.

"You are one very clever lady! You make everything look so easy." Don peeked over Richard's shoulder.

She smiled. "Well, Don, it generally is easy. Not looking makes snooping hard."

"Okay, this is the old list. See, it's dated five years ago. Don, can you access the new list?" Richard scanned the papers.

"You betcha! This is where a photographic memory comes in handy. I saw them preparing the lists today for the meeting." Don sat down at the computer, pushed his hair back over his forehead, stroked his beard and began pecking at the keys.

"Yep, here it is!" He grinned up, proudly. "But this list is dated five years ago, also." Together he and Richard scanned and compared the two lists.

"Well, it looks like there is a difference between the two lists of one M23 land mine, two 4.2-inch M2 mortars and," he whistled, "wow, four M55 rockets. Oh, boy we are in big trouble!"

"Where are the sites they are missing from? Can we go there?" Richard asked quickly.

"Yep, we can go. I'll go with you. But some of this doesn't make sense! They don't have M23 land mines at Aberdeen! At least I didn't think they did." Don stood up. "We know the sites that are missing munitions according to this list. What we don't know is if they are still hidden at those sites or moved somewhere else. We can start at Aberdeen. That's where the land mine is missing according to this list. Which puzzles me. I didn't think there were any chemical weapons at Aberdeen, just the ton containers of chemical agent. Must have found some old buried one. Surely they didn't bring one in and then have it go missing! Why the hell would it be on the first list is the question? Which list is the right one? You'll need me to get in the gate. This is tight security stuff, my friend. Real tight!"

"Good, let me call Harriet first and I'm ready to go.' Richard turned to the phone.

"This sounds pretty serious. Like 'let me call the missus stuff'!" Don eyed him with a half-smile.

Richard turned back to him. "Don, I've known you a long time. And, yes, it is serious. I've asked Harriet to marry me. She said yes. It's to be next week and of course I'll expect you to be there." He grinned.

"Hot damn! You finally bit the bullet! I know that little lady. Met her down in Atlanta. Never thought she'd look at a fella. Let alone a no-good, playin' the field scoundrel like you! That is the best news in a long, long while. You are one lucky dawg. Boy, have I got stories I can tell her! Why so soon? Pappy after you with a gun? Are you sure you want a suspected murderer like me to come to your wedding?" Don was only half kidding.

"No, no gun. Of course I want you. How else can I keep an eye on you." Richard grinned as he dialed.

"Miss Chloe, how about we step out in the hall. I get all misty eyed when I eavesdrop on love birds." Don peeked back around the door, "Does this mean I can inherit your little black book?"

Richard laughed as he shoved aside a huge pile of papers from the desk and the smile froze on his face as his hand uncovered a small cell phone that had been hidden beneath the papers. He glanced at the phone on the desk and lifted the cell phone balancing it in his hand. *Is this Dudley's? That's surprising, it's so heavy*, he thought. Richard picked a nail file from his pocket and went to work on the tiny screws at the upper end of the phone. The top came off to reveal a .22 caliber pistol nestled inside.

CHAPTER FOUR

Richard stuck his head around the door and called out as he pointed to the gun, “Don, Chloe, come back here. Do you know, is this Dudley’s? It’s some kind of a gun!”

“Whew, “ Don whistled. “That’s certainly something new! Never saw one of those before! There’s a guy in this Department who knows everything about kooky guns!” Don picked up the gun with a pen lying nearby. “Be back in a jiff. Want to come Chloe and see the Department in action?” He turned back to Richard. “If this is Dudley’s it’s no big deal. After all, a West Point graduate should be skilled at arms. Why wouldn’t he have a gun?”

“Right. The question is - why wouldn’t he have it with him if he were so scared that he was afraid of a bug in John’s car or house? And where in hell did he get a gun like this?”

“You’re right, he was afraid of someone overhearing his conversation. Wait up, Don. I’m coming with you.” Chloe and Don left Richard alone holding the receiver of the desk phone.

Absent-mindedly he dialed Harriet’s number. After three rings, a disembodied voice said, *No one is available to answer your call. Please leave your number and a message after the signal.* “Hello,

Harriet, I've got to go to Aberdeen Proving Ground. Be back for dinner. Meet you at Gadsby's at eight? Anything I can do for the wedding plans? Is this going to be formal? Do I need to do anything about flowers? Talk about spur of the moment! I'm still in a daze! Happy, but dazed. See you tonight. I love, you. Oh, by the way this is Richard, just in case you had another fella calling about getting married." He smiled as he hung up the phone and started to give the room a more careful scrutiny. *Dudley would have hated this mess, he was such a neat, orderly freak, with his endless lists. Lists, I wonder if he had other lists?* Richard thought. He sat at the desk and started to rummage through the papers. Obviously the intruder had looked at everything lying out and rejected it. A torn slip of paper peeked from under the lamp. Richard picked it up. Three lines were scribbled in Dudley's hand:

small number missing? Why? arms?
nonstockpile? stockpile?
Switch? How?

What the hell does that mean? Thought Richard. He almost threw it away, but he couldn't get the word - 'switch' out of his mind. It had no connection to anything. He stuck the paper in his pocket and glanced at the clock. Don and Chloe were taking their time. He hesitated, then reached for the phone, got his private ATT card out of his wallet, and dialed. "*Better get this out of the way right now*," he thought.

"Allo?" the French accent was heavy.

"Good, Rene, I caught you in. This is Richard Moore. How are you? Am just leaving for Maryland but wanted to get in touch. I know you and Gabriel are coming to the States and I've already asked you to come visit me out on the Potomac, but I was wondering if you could come earlier? You see, I have some really good news. I've met this woman, a really wonderful woman, and we are planning to marry. Well, the thing is we plan to marry next week. Now I know this is sudden, but I'm not getting any younger. Anyway, are you still there?" Richard paused.

"Mon Dieu, yes, I'm still here but such good news. Congratulations. My very best wishes. You are a man with luck or rather I should say your lady is a very lucky woman. When can we meet her? Are you sure you want company at this time? With a wedding to make plans for?"

"That's why I'm calling. I'd like you and Gabriel to come early so you can attend our wedding. Harriet wants a small, family ceremony, so we will not be involved in a great deal of planning and we would still want you to stay with us the following weekend." Richard laughed, "We don't plan a wedding trip. Harriet is a medical doctor, supervising the Smithwick Laboratory until they can get a permanent director. She was with the CDC in Atlanta before she came here. Do say you'll come."

"Mais certainment! We will be delighted. We received an email from John Davis just this morning, so kindly asking us to stay with him. I am going to call him to say that we would accept his generous offer with pleasure. Since that kidnapping of Gabriel in London, I feel much safer to have her staying in a house where the protection is better. When we get to Washington, we can see if you still want visitors for the weekend. I know Gabriel will be pleased, surprised and excited to hear your news. I will tell her this afternoon."

Richard hesitated, thinking he was not so sure of Gabriel's pleasure. "Let me know when you arrive and I'll meet you at the airport. I'll tell John I spoke with you and to plan on your staying with him. Love to Gabriel." As he put the phone down Chloe and Don hurried in.

"McCaully doesn't know if this was Dudley's. Seems these 'cell phone guns' haven't reached the U. S. yet but the FBI and U.S. Customs have been briefed on them. Seems the Dutch police stumbled on a cell-gun during a drug raid in October, then a Croation gun dealer was caught trying to smuggle them into Western Europe. These babies are hard to make, takes a real expert. They think the guns were made in Yugosolvia. Under the digital face is a .22 caliber pistol capable of firing four rounds in succession by touching what appears to be a standard keypad You load the gun by twisting the face half-way, the .22 caliber rounds go in the top half under the screen and the lower half of the keypad holds the firing pins. Press the keypad and the bullets go out through the antenna. Voila. I'd call this a lady's gun."

"Exactly what does that mean, 'a lady's gun'?" Chloe bristled.

Richard laughed, "That's a gun in the hand of a lady!"

"Why would Dudley have a lady's gun?" Don ignored Chloe. "And the only other lady, besides Chloe here, involved in this committee work is Jo Ferguson. McCaully did say the FBI had been briefed on them. Do you know, did Dudley have a gun on him when they found the body?" Don plopped down in a vacant chair. He had put on a little weight and was feeling the effect of the stairs.

"I haven't had a chance to check what was on him. It just happened last night and I spent all my free time since then reading up on these CT's for the meeting today. But it's possible one or two people could be involved in this. The person who bugged Dudley's phone could have left the cell phone, or the person who ransacked his office could have overlooked or forgotten the cell phone. Look, Chloe, could you check if Dudley had a gun with him and also, Don, could you get her some background checks on the people at the meeting today?"

"Sure, I'll ask my secretary to assemble files for you right now." Don rose groaning from the chair. "For some reason, my back has been killing me this week."

"We'll walk down to your office with you and then maybe you'd like to drive out to Aberdeen with me and see what's what there." Richard turned to Chloe, "Could you meet John at his house this afternoon? I'll go there as soon as we get back and we can compare our findings. John should have information on the army's computer lists by then. Come on, Don, if you creak along like that, I'll never give you all my old phone numbers."

"Look, Buddy, this is not a case of would I like to go to Aberdeen with you. It's a case of: you don't get in unless I either go with you or see you have all the faxes, etc.. I don't think you realize the intense security at these CT depots. You don't just go waltzing in. You're dealing with the army here and the tightest of Homeland Security." He huffed as they walked along. "First, I'll have them make out passes for us to get in. Then they fax them down to the base so we can pick them up when we get there. Do you have any idea of the size of that site? My God, that place has twelve national guard units; Baltimore only has eight! The U.S. Army Garrison Aberdeen Proving Ground manages and operates the whole shebang. Aberdeen has

73,000 acres with 2,200 buildings. So it may take a while locating a specific place. Here we are. Richard, this is my secretary, Jack Nichols. Jack, would you fill out faxes to get us into Aberdeen and hold everything I have for this afternoon?"

"Yes, Sir." A sprightly young man in his early twenties searched the papers on his desk. "Aha! Here you go." He handed a page to both Richard and Don. "Please fill out all the personal stuff and I'll enter the type of security, company/organization etc. and fax it off. You can't take it with you as the saying goes. That applies here. The request has to be sent ahead. You haven't been there yet, have you, Sir? You're in for a treat."

"No, this is my maiden voyage. Thanks, Jack. Bring that in my office and we'll get this thing started." Don nodded to Richard, who followed him into a rather spacious set of rooms.

"Not bad, not bad at all for a poor boy from Georgia." Richard surveyed the office with a small bathroom to the side. "What's with the 'sir' from the youngster outside? I thought he was going to salute."

"He's not gotten over his West Point training. Everyone here has had some kind of army training and boy, are these guys close. It's like a clique, an old-boys club rolled into one. Come on hurry up. Fill that damn thing out. We've still got a drive ahead of us."

"Do you want me to get a driver for you, Sir?" Jack poked his head around the door.

"No thanks, Jack. But could you get me a map and some instructions on the damn place?" Jack disappeared and Don plopped into his chair with a sigh.

"Take exit #77 and Maryland Route 24 South." Richard was reading from the map on his lap. They had both been silent as Don maneuvered the Washington traffic to get on to I-95. "So, I understand we're supposedly checking the mix-up in serial numbers on one-ton containers of chemicals. Do they have chemical weapons at Aberdeen, also? Didn't you say the land mine was here?"

"According to one of the lists that Dudley had, Aberdeen just has stock-piled chemicals in containers; then on the other list there is this one supposedly-missing land mine. But it may be non-stockpile. They found 40 non-stockpile munitions in 1994. God knows what all is buried there." Don leaned back in his seat. "I'll be so glad to get off I-95."

"Tell me about Aberdeen," Richard said.

"Well, to begin with, it's the oldest active proving ground, started in 1917. At that time, they had to move their weapon testing out of the populated area at Sandy Hook, New Jersey and so picked the western shore of the Chesapeake. Ironic isn't it? Now they are located 21 miles north of Baltimore on the megalopolis corridor from New York to Washington! From the frying pan into the fire! Talk about heavy population area! They've been making and testing weapons from World War I up to now.

"The site has two areas: the northern or Aberdeen Area and the southern sector, the Edgewood Area, used to be called the Edgewood Arsenal. That's where we'll be going. The Bush River separates the two areas. Edgewood was established as a chemical weapons research, development and testing facility. While President Roosevelt said we would not use chemical weapons offensively in World War II, what he meant was, we would use them defensively. But you knew that. So, we researched and developed chemical weapons. The Army Chemical and Biological Defense Command (CBDCOM) has the responsibility for the stockpile of chemical agents and munitions, non-stockpile weapons and munitions, etc. More then fifty groups of stockpile exist at Aberdeen. The term 'non-stockpile' includes a hell of a lot. You see, the U.S. has nine sites designated 'stockpile' and all the rest – munitions, chemicals, you name it- are lumped under the 'non-stockpile'. The person in charge of all this is the Program Manager for the Chemical Materials Agency. They got this agency by combining the old Chemical Demilitarization Program (CDP) and the Soldier Biological and Chemical Command (SBCCOM). Honest to God, it's like vegetable soup! So the Program Manager, who's in Washington, reports to the under secretary of defense. The guy in charge at Aberdeen is Colonel Green.

"The army's been using the 500-acre wooded site of the Bush River Area now for storage of bulk chemical agents and wastes. It used to be used for training, testing and disposal as well. As I said, the area has had a lot of trouble with buried non-stockpile chemical weapons like Sarin, mustard, and VX."

John, looking at the map and instructions, interrupted him. "We go four miles through an unmanned military gate entrance, at the 1st stoplight turn left on Magnolia Road. Okay, I'm with you on the map your secretary gave us. Now turn left at the next light onto Wise Road and it says here to follow to DRMO BLDG. #E-1890. There it is, a large white building on the left. Pull into the parking lot over there on the left. Now what?"

"We're suppose to pick up passes if they got our faxes in that building. I'm using your college connection as a professor, not the Noir connection, in all introductions. Can you imagine the uproar that would cause here, a secret society?" Don heaved himself out of the car and hobbled in with Richard holding the door. "I'm Donald Mozley, Homeland Security and my colleague Professor Richard Moore. My secretary faxed our pass information this morning. We have a rather limited time frame."

"Yes, we received your fax. Please go into room 12B and wait. I'll prepare your passes," A very efficient twenty-year old blond with a no-nonsense- attitude replied.

"Can we hurry it up?" Don asked.

"We will go as quickly as rules allow," the blond explained coldly and turned back to her computer.

Fifteen minutes later the blond returned. "Here are your passes. Go to the right when you come to a fork in the road. Those without passes go left."

"You take the high road...," Don tried to sing. The blond stared at him coldly.

As they got back in the car, Don commented, "Why is it the military have so little humor?

"Maybe because staying alive in a war is not funny. Oh, My God, look at this long concrete maze will you? Don, see right ahead of us? If I'm not mistaken, we are looking at a manned machine gun aimed right at us. I suggest we not make any false move. Thank God we're in an official army-marked car.

Twenty minutes later, passes in hand, Don and Richard were ushered into the office of the director of Aberdeen. A man in his forties with wrinkled face and flapping jowls arose from a cluttered desk. "Good morning, Gentlemen. I'm Colonel Green. How can I help you?"

Richard was impressed with his sharp eyes and firm handshake. Green's stance was upright but not rigid, his eyes kind as well as keen. While Richard waited for Don to speak, since he had initiated the interview, he couldn't help comparing this soldier with Major Dowell to the latter's disadvantage.

Don came right to the point. "I believe you've been informed that we are here to try and straighten out some mix-up with serial numbers and locations of chemical containers. Professor Moore and I wanted to view your storage arrangements and methods of serial identification. We are on the same Department of Homeland Security Committee as Major Dowell." At the mention of Dowell's name, Green's face darkened, for just a moment. He was obviously too politic or aware of army conduct to make a comment, but the look spoke volumes.

"Yes, we heard you were working on this. Please be seated. I'll go over some of the background of our facility, then perhaps you would like to see the installations. We'll begin with the liquid mustard agent often mistakenly referred to as a gas. The Chemical Agent Storage Yard or CASEY at the Edgewood Area of Aberdeen Proving Ground was built in 1941 to store bulk mustard agents. We have 1,818 one-ton containers, not all full. The ton containers with mustard agent are stacked eight on the bottom row and seven on the middle row. The empty containers on the top row protect the bottom and middle rows. These ton containers rest on railroad ties and are held in place with steel cables.

"A two-man team conducts a visual entry monitoring known as a first entry monitoring. The chemical agent mustard or HD is the only chemical agent we store at CASEY. We visually inspect the valves and plugs of each ton container regularly. CASEY has ten chemical agent monitoring systems located at the perimeter of the yard going 24 hours a day and chemical agent sample ports on the other side of the inner fence. Signs outside CASEY shows what's stored and what you'll need in the way of protective gear to enter."

"May we visit the area?" Don asked.

"Yes, of course. That's why you came. Please don't take offense, but we did a background search to identify you as soon as we got your fax, just routine." For just a minute Green eyed them, then the moment passed. "Come with me. You'll need a health check, just the usual, blood pressure, doctor interview, etc. and then they will fit you with a gas mask if you want to handle or touch the containers."

"Could I use a phone, Colonel? It's a personal call if that's allowed. I had made an appointment for this afternoon and I can see this will take longer then I expected." Richard stood up as he spoke.

"Indeed. You can use the phone in my office. Dial nine. We have a direct line to Washington. I must warn you, we monitor all calls. I'll get Mozley started on his health check." Green was out of his seat and through the door before Don had risen.

"That's all I need to make this a piss-awful day, " Don moaned as he followed Green out the door.

Richard waited for a several minutes before he could secure a line and then for the connection. Again, an answering machine greeted him. He spoke after the buzzer, "Hello, John. Look we're going to be here a lot later then we thought. Probably not get home until the wee hours, so could we meet in the morning and compare notes? Would you call Harriet and tell her to cancel dinner. Great way to start off the wedding plans isn't it? Got to run." From the other corridor he could hear Don swearing. Richard followed the sound.

"What do you mean I'm in poor shape and what the hell do you mean shave my beard?" Don was sitting partially clad on an examining table. A six-foot nurse, stout of limb and short of temper was glaring down on him.

"You're blood pressure is off the scale, you're muscle tone is nothing, your pulse is racing and your blood sugar is much too high. Probably working up to diabetes. The only normal part of your examination is your temperature. In case of an explosion, you'd never make it to the door. State Department connection or not, they shouldn't let you enter a danger area. You can go in and see the doctor now, if you don't have heart failure getting off the table. Your wife should be strung up for letting you get so out of shape."

"I'm not married. So you can only blame me. And what the hell do you mean shave my beard? Do you know how long I was growing this?" Don was getting purple in the face.

The phrase 'not married' caused an ever so slight change of tone to her voice. "You have to wear a gas mask and it does not seal perfectly with a beard or moustache. So if you don't shave, you can't enter!" She went to help Don off the table. Insulted, he brushed her aside and tried to get off by himself. Richard coughed to keep from laughing as Don turned on his stomach, lowered himself to the floor and stomped off. Richard was even more amused when, after Don had left, the nurse only took his blood pressure and checked his heart rate and signaled him to leave.

Two hours later, an industrious sergeant ushered them into another room. "I'm going to instruct you in the use of the atropine autoinject packs or the Mark I. While you don't really need these with mustard, the Colonel thought you'd be interested in what you'd need if you were entering a nerve gas installation for instance. Something to occupy your time until they can get someone to show you around. You'd have three of these Mark I's in your fanny pack. You can wear your own clothes as long as you're not going into the most hazardous areas." As he began his long lecture and explanation, Richard looked around the building they were in. No glass windows. The glass would probably be dangerous if an explosion occurred and give no protection. Thick walls surrounded them, again a protection feature.

Another hour and fifteen minutes was spent learning and adjusting the equipment. Finally another sergeant appeared. "So, now lets take a walk around CASEY and then we'll go to the bunkers that are left over from WWII." They stepped out into the full sun and were almost blinded. Following the leader in a line-like fashion, the sergeant led them through several wire fences. Watch towers were visible in several corners.

As far as he could see were piles of one-ton containers, piled three deep. *Good Lord, how could they possibly keep track of them. I'm amazed they have only lost so few weapons. But then these are not weapons, just chemical agents. I can't wait to see the weapons!,*

Richard thought to himself. "Do you have chemical weapons as well as the ton containers of mustard?" Richard asked.

"No, not that we know of, only the mustard agent. Of course what's buried here is anyone's...."

The sergeant was interrupted by a high wail of a siren. Men came running in all directions. The sergeant turned to them abruptly. "I'm sorry, we must go back inside. That is an alert. A warning! Please hurry!" He jogged them back to the building nearest them, several down from the one that they had just left. "Please wait here in the lobby. I'll come back as soon as I find out what has happened." He stopped an enlisted man running past. "You, stay with these two." He was leaving even as he spoke.

"So what do we do now?" Don was completely out of sorts.

"We wait here. Maybe that nice nurse will come back and tell you what you should tell your wife to do for you, if you ever get a wife." Richard scanned the room. Not a magazine, nothing. He inspected his sample fanny pack and started fiddling with the autoinjector. When he looked over, Don had gone sound asleep in his chair. Outside Richard could hear more sirens, shouted orders and running feet even through the thick walls. The young soldier was standing nervously rocking back and forth on his feet.

"Why don't you sit down? We're not about to make a run for it." Richard smiled at him.

The youngster grinned back. "You all must be pretty high muckety-muck to get in here, civilians and all."

"Where are you from? The accent says Tennessee." Richard inquired leisurely.

"Yes, Sir, Nashville. But I don't think I should be talking to you. I mean, I'm not sure and I don't want to get into trouble." He blushed.

"Well, I don't want you to, so I'll just sit here and stare at the wall." Richard tried not to notice the awkward young man and concentrated on the white-washed, army regulation walls and listened to Don snore.

When the sergeant returned, he was accompanied by Colonel Green. The slamming of the door woke Don who sat up with a start. Green spoke quietly, "Look, I'm sorry about all this. Something of a mess! Please come into my office and I will brief you both. You are dismissed, Sergeant." Both the sergeant and the guarding soldier saluted, turned, and left.

Silently Don and Richard followed Green out of the building and back to the one they first entered and down the hall. Groups of soldiers were standing around whispering. Outside sirens still wailed and they could hear hurrying feet in adjacent corridors. Seated back in the office, Green cleared his throat. "Well, this is certainly an unusual visit. First, I want you to know you are safe. What happened has nothing to do with the neutralization process. That was obviously our greatest concern. In April of 2003, we began the process of destroying the bulk stockpile of mustard agent; we've even accelerated the destruction by two years. Because of 9/11 and threat of terrorist attacks, we have a new project, "Speedy Neut" that changes the original neutralization process. We're going to destroy the mustard first. We have an impressive, dedicated team of 400 people working on this. Mustard is a syrup, a blister compound that looks like molasses. It has been safely stored and monitored here for 60 years. We've been working 24/7 to get this neutralizing set up.

"When the sirens went off we were afraid something had gone wrong with the neutralization process. What happened was that they found a body." John and Richard sat forward. "It was one of our workers. They found him behind a storage building. We were afraid he had been affected by the chemical agent. He hadn't. Someone had hit him over the head with a pipe. The reason I was so long getting back to you is that this particular man was supposed to have just been admitted to an old bunker storage unit that we had just discovered. Thought those bunkers were all gone until we found this one. At least someone with his I.D. had entered. We let as few persons as possible go in at one time for safety reasons. They wear a high-hazard protection suit and it is very hard to recognize the person inside with our monitoring systems. Anyway we have apprehended this imposter in the bunker and he in undergoing questioning now. I might as well tell you, because you'll find out anyway, he had somehow dragged in a landmine with him, a weapon that is not listed in any of our lists of weapons. I'm sure the Homeland Security

Department will have people crawling all over the place by tonight." Only the strictest discipline kept him from saying more.

"What would happen if a land mine went off in the bunker?" Richard asked finally.

"It's hard to say," Green answered hesitantly. "Obviously, it would kill the person in the bunker and probably several near-by in the observation rooms. Everything is remotely monitored by computers. Of course the munitions would explode and the chemicals would be released, but we have trained teams to handle that. What I just can't understand is why anyone would go to all the trouble to get a land mine into that old bunker, a land mine imported from somewhere else, I assume. No easy feat, to go to so much trouble to do such limited damage. So many questions: where did the mine come from, was it part of an old stockpile from long ago located here, if not, how did they get it in, you saw the security, and why so much trouble for so little return?"

"Either it was very poorly planned, which is unlikely seeing how much they have achieved, or there is a larger more complex plan," Don mused. "Could it have been from an old buried munitions dump?"

"Possibly, but not likely," Green answered.

"Who else of the Committee from Homeland Security that Don and I are on have visited here?" Richard asked quietly.

Green turned sharply. "I'll have to consult the files but to my knowledge Armad Beel, Jack Bancroft, and Jo Ferguson. I guess I remember them because Armad is of Moslem descent and after 9/11 I must admit I am prejudiced about the Moslem element, probably unjustly so. Seemed like a steady, hard-working chap. I liked him. And I always remember FBI and CIA involvement, besides Jo is a very attractive woman and I'm not that old! Jack seemed to find her attractive, also" He smiled, the first that day. Then remembering the serious situation he added, "Major Dowell doesn't come here often, if ever. He is probably going to retire. Dowell was passed over for a promotion, don't know why he didn't get it, but he seems angry about the slight. Being the rigid, army-by-the-book man that he likes to think himself, he'll never make a fuss. Just retire and take a nice, highly paid job in some successful business. Dowell spends most of his time at the base at Tooele out in Utah. I can check the files and get back to you about how often and when they visited."

"Thank you, I'd appreciate that. Now, is it okay for us to take a closer look at the chemical ton containers or do you want us to come back?" Don asked, secretly hoping he'd say 'come back.'

Green was of the 'damn the torpedoes full speed ahead school' so unfortunately for Don, Green said, "Of course, since you're here and all ready, I think we can continue. No chemicals were released. I'll call the sergeant and you can get on with it." Don groaned and avoided Richard's smile.

A sergeant entered the room and handed Green a paper. After scanning the sheet, Green looked up. "The man who died, worked in the old bunker and had a legitimate badge. He was killed by a blow from behind with, we believe, a pipe that we found nearby. He was friends with the man whom we apprehended in the bunker, the same man who was trying to set off a landmine. This suspected killer worked on the construction crew that supplies oil to the base. It's delivered in large tankers. He knew the victim. Seems they were grew up in the same neighborhood, friends since grade school. Some friend!"

"Do they have an address for this interloper they found in the bunker?" Richard asked.

"Yes, in D.C. I'll get a copy for you, if you wish, of all the information we have on him. I'm sure FBI and CIA have people out there combing the place right now. Please follow me now and we'll finish your tour."

CHAPTER FIVE

"Papa, are you busy? Could you help me? I can't get my case closed!" Gabriel laughed as she tried to sit on her suitcase and zip it at the same time.

"I'm coming, Ma Cherie." Rene stopped at the door. "Mon, Dieu! How many suitcases do you have? We will only be gone three weeks not three years!" He smiled indulgently. "I was going to ask why you packed so soon, we don't leave until next week, but as it turns out, it's a good thing you did. That was Richard Moore on the phone. He has asked us to come a week early."

"I knew it! He can't stand to be separated from me a moment longer. He has to see me!" Gabriel laughed triumphantly.

"Hardly that, you little teaser, he wants us to come early because he is getting married and he wants us to attend the wedding." Rene, engrossed in closing the suitcase, missed the shock on her face or her turning pale, and he continued, "I said that we would be imposing to stay at his house next weekend if he is involved with the great romance. Did I tell you that John Davis emailed us an invitation to stay with him at his family's home in Georgetown? I am afraid he is smitten with you. I plan to call and accept his kind offer. I'd feel so much safer with you staying in a private home then in a hotel after that horrible episode in London. That way I can keep a closer eye on you. There, the suitcase is closed! Fini!" He looked up, "Ma Cheri, what is it? You are so pale! Are you going to faint? Here, sit down. You have overdone yourself with all this packing and shopping! I should not have mentioned that London situation. What was I thinking of? Suzanne," he called, "Vite! Vite! Your mistress needs help." He took Gabriel and half-carried, half-dragged her to a couch. "It is so warm in here, vite, vite, ouvrez la fenetre, Suzanne!" Rene sat down at Gabriel's side.

The maid came to the door, surveyed the scene, and silently opened the window, then went to the bath for a towel dipped in cool water. Being a very perceptive young woman, she remained silent, having overheard the conversation in the room next to where she was cleaning. She did not comment that the cause of her mistress's pallor might be shock not heat. Suzanne applied the cool cloths to Gabriel's forehead and neck.

"Suzanne, stop it! Papa, don't fuss! I'm all right, just a little tired. Do leave me a while and let me rest." She pushed the cool towels aside, avoiding Suzanne's eyes. "No, wait. Tell me what Richard had to say about his wedding." She tugged at his sleeve as he rose to leave. "When is it? Who is she?"

"Ah," Rene laughed, "women and curiosity! Nothing overcomes that! It's to be next week and she is a medical doctor. They met while he was working on a case. Apparently the decision was of a sudden."

"Oh, good, a medical doctor! She must be quite old! She has obviously vamped him and he is acting hastily! If we can get there early enough, I can make him change his mind and stop this horrible wedding!" Gabriel laughed delightedly.

"What's this? What are you saying?" Rene scanned the face she turned to him, then true to his diplomatic calling, he remembered Suzanne. "That will be all, Suzanne. Leave us." He waited until the young girl had departed, then turned toward Gabriel. "What is this? What madness are you saying? Richard Moore is a dear friend and old enough to be your father," at the word 'father,' he immediately hesitated and looked away. "But you are joking, right?"

"Papa, I'm old beyond my years, I've heard you say so many times. Richard has been here to visit us and we to visit him. He's been to all my parties and always seemed so interested in me. Now if he married me, we could be close like a family, just we three, once we get rid of that awful woman who has hypnotized him."

Rene stared at her unbelievingly, rose slowly and walked to the open window. For untold moments he stood as if transfixed, staring out into the night. Painfully he turned and came back to the couch and Gabriel, seating himself beside her he took her hand. "Ma Cherie, I must tell you something that all my life I have wished I would never have to tell. But first, I want you to know I loved your mother very much and I believe she loved me, also. Richard is not only old enough to be your father, he is your father."

Gabriel withdrew her hand and stared at him. "What are you saying? Richard…?"

"I loved your mother when she was a little girl, much younger then you. As she grew into womanhood, she was an angel of beauty, laughter and happiness surrounded her. So lively, such spirit. I was much older then she and I fear she was awed by the attention of an older man. We were married and for a while were ecstatically happy. Then she became restless, bored, wanted adventure. She heard of the Noir, a secret organization. Somehow, I think she knew your grandmother, Chloe, whom she worshipped was a secret agent. It sounded so glamorous, so exciting! She was after me night and day until finally I agreed for her to join. She met Richard there and I believe, though she never said, they were lovers. When she returned and told me her baby was mine, I accepted it because I wanted to believe it. Then after three years, she went back to the Noir and died in an ambush. Richard brought the news. As you grew, I could see him in you, his eyes, and his chin. At first I hated you, then I saw your mother's likeness in you, also, and felt that I had her back again, her laugh, her enthusiasm, her stubbornness. I felt if I acknowledged him as your father I would lose you as well as Marie all over again, so I stayed silent. Can you understand?"

During the whole recital, Gabriel had stared at him frozen. When he reached for her hand, she shook it off. Her scream startled him. "Lies! Lies! You're saying this to keep me away from Richard!"

"My little one, can you possibly imagine in your wildest dreams that I would make up such a story?" Never had she seen such sadness as his face reflected, but his despair did not reach her.

"Why have you never spoken of this before? Who else knows of this secret? Obviously Richard. Grandmamma? John? I am humiliated! Everyone laughing behind my back. Poor little Gabriel, in love with her father! I hate you!"

"Of course Richard knows and probably your Grandmother. I don't know about John. No one is laughing at you. Gabriel, I have been with you every moment of your life. Am I less a father because you don't have my genes? When I thought I had lost you in London I went mad! Can you not understand this?" Rene was pleading.

She ignored him, lost in her own thoughts. Quickly she reviewed the last few moments and they seemed like years quickly putting so much into perspective. Her emotions changing as rapidly as her thoughts: love, hate, humiliation, and finally, revenge. *So, John doesn't know, maybe? He's crazy about me. He's always near Richard. I could be, too if I married John. I could make Richard feel guilty for never telling me, for making my mother die, or letting me fall in love with him, for humiliating me. All of this trouble is his fault.* Reluctantly she looked at Rene's bowed head. *First, I must get to America. Father will never let me go if he senses I want revenge.* So with great effort she changed her face as carefully as if she were donning a new dress. She put her hand on Rene's arm. "I'm sorry I said I hate you. It's just such a shock. I still can't believe it. Don't worry, Papa, I know that you will always do what is best for me. You will always be my papa. And I will be good when we go to America. I really do love you, Papa." To her surprise, she found she meant it. Rene's tears stirred a feeling of guilt.

Richard held the phone close to his ear to keep out the noise of the street. He stood with one hand over the other ear to try and hear. "John, I'm back in D.C. Could you and Chloe pick me up? Lots to tell. We can catch up in the car. Got to go to an apartment up on 13th street. Yes, I'll tell you when you get here. I'm on the corner of the Nebraska Avenue Center at the entrance of the Department of

Homeland Security. How long before you can pick me up? Okay, see you in thirty minutes, traffic permitting."

He folded his phone and put it back in his pocket. "Don, I appreciate your putting me up last night. It was so late when we got back I dreaded that drive out to Potomac. Want to join me for breakfast in this coffee shop here on the corner? We have about a half hour before John and Chloe can get here."

Don nodded and headed for the door. "Do we have to talk this early in the morning?"

"I'll talk, you listen and scowl if you disagree." Richard laughed and headed for an empty table. "Black coffee for both of us," he said to the waitress as he took a menu from her outstretched hand. Turning to Don he said, "I couldn't sleep last night and I kept going over what we have so far. We've all been thinking the mix-up in serial numbers was just that. But is it more serious as you suggested to Green? We know now that some weapons are missing, but disruptive as their use is, could it be something is going on a larger scale?" As the waitress returned, he looked at the menu, "Want anything to eat?"

"First things first, " Don replied. Turning to the waitress he smiled for the first time all morning, "I'll have two eggs over, sausage, pancakes and large orange juice. Oh, and lots of syrup."

She turned to a smiling Richard, "And you, Sir?"

"An English muffin, please." Richard handed her the menu.

"Is that all? Just a muffin?" Mozley queried.

"Don, remember that huge seafood dinner we had about 1 a.m. after we got back from Aberdeen? I'm still stuffed. And speaking of Aberdeen, what did you think of Green?"

"Solid army, good man." Don sipped his coffee. "But I have a feeling there is no love lost between him and Dowell. Now there, meaning Dowell, is one big pain in the ass. Did you get the fire fight between him and Jo Ferguson?"

Richard nodded. "And back to my original question: is something else bigger looming with this CT thing?"

"Do we have to talk shop so early?" Don groaned, "Okay, okay! I think, and this is a gut feeling, that the land mine is more then just a bungled job. It's going to get a lot of media attention and will take a lot of time investigating. Then let's say they pull another 'terrorist attack' with one of the mortars. I would guess the rockets would be used at the last moment right before whatever big thing is going down. The military will find they are all tied up stifling these attacks with probably significant civilian casualties and political finger-pointing to do much about another CT problem. All of this is surmise. While Green didn't say as much, I feel he was thinking along these lines. What do the military call it…'a diversion action'?" Don looked up as the waitress put the plate before him. "That was fast!" She smiled and set the other plate at Richard's place.

"Could you bring me the check?" Richard asked. Then turning to Don, "Now we're talking a big operation. Who has the money and know how to do all that's required? For what purpose? You saw the security! It would take a lot of planning to mess with the army. Hell, it would be easier and cheaper to get a lab and make weapons on your own." Richard spread the jam on his muffin.

"True. But it's also a very dangerous game this 'doing it yourself'. You've been reading the lethal nature of this stuff. Whoever works with it ends up first drawer in the morgue. Of course, with all the suicide bombers, what have they got to lose? And not only do they end up with a bevy of beauties in Nirvana or wherever, but all their families are taken care of and will remember the guys fondly at family reunions. But how do you explain a lot of dead bodies to nosy authorities? And how do you transport chemicals wherever you want to take them? No, it's much better to steal the stuff already made and boxed as it were. But what if it's not the nutty Muslim terrorists doing this?" Don attacked his stack of pancakes with gusto.

Richard glanced out the window and saw John pulling up to the curb. "Oops, here they are. Got to run." He threw a couple of bills on the table. "Appreciate it, Don. See you."

"Thanks, John. Hi Chloe," Richard spoke as he flung open the door and managed to sit as John pulled away from the curb.

"Sorry for the fast pull away, but a meter maid was three cars back and I was in a 'no parking' zone. So what time did you get home?"

"I didn't. Spent the night with Don. While we were at Aberdeen, a man was killed, his badge taken and the interloper tried to set off a landmine in one of the old-time bunkers. We didn't get home until late. I think the mine was the one on that list. Whoever they are, they are moving fast. What have you two found?" Richard fastened his seat belt.

"First, could you give me an address? I mean where are we going?" John had circled the block.

"Oops, sorry. I got the address of the interloper from Colonel Green who manages Aberdeen. It's in the northeast section 13th avenue." Richard smiled and nodded to Chloe in the backseat.

Chloe laughed. "The most dangerous assignment of this whole escapade might be going into that address. Do you know the section? Muggers up there go out in twos for protection." She continued more seriously, "I'll go first with what I found out. Yes, Dudley did have a gun on him when he died. Dr. Patterson found huge amounts of VX in his throat where the umbrella tip penetrated. That's why he went so fast. Sorry, John. If this helps any, he felt very little pain as soon as it entered his neck because some sort of local anesthetic was also found. Since the VX was in his throat and went right into the artery, no way could he have been saved." John drove with his face set, staring straight ahead and went a little faster.

"I got the background on everyone and will give it to you in abbreviated form. You can read their whole folio when you have time," Chloe continued. "Armad Beel was born in Oakland, California, mother a biology professor, Dad a lawyer. Graduated from Berkeley magna cum laude in computer science. Lives within his means in Georgetown and has a girl friend but I haven't found her name yet. Follows the Moslem religion.

"Major Dowell has been in the army twenty-five years. Graduated from a small community college in Ohio. Never married, but had multiple affairs. His address is Aberdeen, but he spends very little time there. Prefers to take on duty at Tooele. Goes there whenever possible. Some of his old army buddies live at the base. Hangs out with construction men at the plant. Passed over for a promotion and here the details are rather murky, different stories: fight in a bar a long time ago, insult an officer, lots of little things mentioned. Not too well liked. No religious affiliation."

"I think you turn here, John. This does look like a rather dangerous section. Thank God we're here during the day." Richard checked the street sign.

Chloe took up her recital again, "Jack Bancroft and Jo Ferguson both graduated from the University of Michigan. She's from Ann Arbor and he's from Cleveland. Apparently he's had a crush on her all through college. Both majored in political science. He's a Republican and she's a Democrat. Isn't it amazing the information we have on people? She's been following Dudley around ever since Jack introduced them. Dudley didn't know she was alive. Both live in Chevy Chase, neither lives beyond their means. He alone and she with a sorority sister."

"Hold it, Chloe. I think we're here. Yep, North 13th street. That one-story brick building. I asked Don to tell the guard they have posted at the door to let us in." Richard jumped out and held the door for Chloe. The brick apartment building had seen better days, some windows were boarded up where cracked glass was visible, other were just boards. A few had rusty window air-conditioners that looked like they no longer worked. Garbage cans scattered over the sidewalk were attracting a few stray cats. The smell signaled pick-up was long past due. Three cracked concrete steps led to a red door, or at least it may have been red thirty years ago.

John parked his car, locked the door and patted the fender as if he might not see it again. "Lead on McDuff" he called to Richard.

A single light bulb on a cord gave little light in the narrow hall. Richard walked to the back of the hall and knocked on 12D. A tall man in uniform opened the door and blocked the entrance. "Yeah?"

"Hi. I'm Richard Moore. Don Mozley said we could look around."

"Could I see some ID, Sir?" The hefty young man kept his place in the door.

"Yes, of course." Richard pulled out his driver's license and his ID card that he had left from his visit to the Homeland Security committee meeting. Chloe and John each handed him a driver's license.

"Okay. He called you were coming. Doubt you'll find anything. The military are very thorough and they really combed this place. Even took the frig contents."

"Look, if there's no food, why don't you go out and get something to eat. We'll wait 'til you get back. Do you want John here to go with you? Tough neighborhood." Richard smiled. "By the way, this is John Davis and Chloe Manning." He held out his hand.

"Lieutenant Mitchell, Sir. I'd really appreciate getting some grub. I've been on duty since three this morning. I grew up in a neighborhood much like this. I don't think I'll need an escort, but thanks anyway." He grinned.

Chloe appraised his six-foot-four muscled form. "I agree. Take your time and get a meal and something to carry you through until you can get some relief. Believe me, we won't take anything here." She glanced around at the meager furnishings.

"Right, I really appreciate this Sir, Ma'm." Mitchell couldn't leave fast enough.

"I always thought they paid construction workers pretty well. Didn't you say this guy was on a construction crew?" John surveyed the room gloomily.

"Nope. He delivered oil to the base. Here's the stuff Green e-mailed me. No relatives, no record of schools attended or places lived. Sounds like an illegal immigrant." Richard read from the paper in his hand.

"And they let guys like that on an army base with deadly chemicals in containers! Why in God's name?" John flung himself in a rickety dining chair.

"They let him on because he's part of the construction company which is supposed to vet their people. He was just cleared to be around the civilian houses. Nobody knows how he got over on the other side of the base." He stopped and looked at an old clock on the side table and checked his watch from habit. "Right on time. Bet it has 7-day works. Look, I'll take this room and you do the kitchen. Chloe, would you check the bedroom?"

Ten minutes later they were all back in the living room. "Not much to check here. Furniture isn't upholstered, no pictures. Nothing. Mitchell was right about the fridge…no food. The military probably didn't have much else to take. Richard, are you listening to me?" John spoke irritably.

Richard sat staring at the clock on a table by the door, an oak, wooden wind-up clock of the kind popular fifty years ago. "While that clock probably isn't valuable, it's so out of keeping with the rest of this apartment. Have you ever noticed that the tick and tock of a clock are even sounds if the clock keeps good time as this one seems to? Yet this clock has a pendulum that bumps on one side and not the other. See, listen to the thud." Chloe and John both stopped and stared at the clock. Richard rose and went to the table, opened the front of the clock and lifted out the brass pendulum. As he did his hand brushed the side of the cabinet and a piece of paper fell down. Then he reached up behind the clock works to feel the back of the cabinet. Gingerly he dislodged a small black book taped to the back wall. He replaced the pendulum and when he tapped it, the clock started again. The door stood open. He smiled, "See, you can hear the difference. What have we here? An address book! John, check this out while I read this scrap of paper. If Mitchell comes back, hide it."

John rapidly thumbed through the book. "Oh, boy! Here's Armad Beel listed and there's another name in parenthesis below his - Louise Wiggins. I don't recognize any other names."

"Well, his writing is bad, but on the scrap of paper it looks like Tabor Rester with a Chicago address and a date. The date is this Friday. We don't have a lot of time." Richard looked up.

"Things don't look too good for Beel, do they? You know I really liked the guy. He certainly knows computers. It seems that the army is redoing some of its software- tracking CT's and at the same time Hazardous Substance Management System or HSMS is redoing software for some army bases. All this was written up in an Army HSMS Newsletter. You know how sensitive the army is to anything to do with the environment now, even publish a newsletter keeping everybody informed. Well, it looks to us like somehow the two updates accessed the same minor file and caused a cross-over of a couple of spaces, so all the numbers of the ton-canisters are right but out of sync. Armad still has some checking to see if this is what happened. Does this mean we can just concentrate on the missing weapons and forget about the ton-canisters and do you all think Beel appears to be in deep shit?" John pocketed the book and turned toward Richard.

"When we were searching Dudley's office, I found a scrap of paper that the burglar had overlooked. It had several things scribbled on it. I have it here in my pocket." He began searching through his coat. "Here we are:

small number missing? Why? arms?
nonstockpile? NO! stockpile?
Switch? How?

Dudley had a very orderly mind. Apparently he was worried about the same thing Green voiced yesterday, 'why go to so much work for a relatively small return?' My guess, and this is just a hunch, is that he had discarded the missing weapons idea and was concentrating on the stockpile. I don't know what 'switch' means. But if stealing the weapons was a diversion tactic, then the real action could be at some other military site then the ones involved in the weapon theft. I don't know about disregarding the ton-canisters. Could they be the main event and someone slipped up, that's why the numbers are out of order? Does this make sense?" Richard walked over to the one grimy window and surveyed the street.

"Following that line of reasoning, then the weapons that are missing, at least the landmine, was a nonstockpile item at Aberdeen, which means the rest of the missing weapons could be either nonstockpile or stockpile. So if they are a diversion and we find them, we can eliminate the sites where they were found." Chloe rocked back and forth in her chair. "John, I'm afraid things don't look good for Beel. The one thing in his favor is that he's been going to Aberdeen, according to what Richard found out from Green, and we've just eliminated that site from suspicion, if Richard's theory is correct. I might point out that there are seven other sites with CWs and one with CTs. We don't have a lot of time to find any special one"

"Well, right now it looks like we should head for Chicago and look up Mr. Tabor Rester. We're going to have to get air transport quickly. Mozley might be able to work that out. I'd like to suggest that we bring along the FBI and CIA on this. Why don't we ask

Jo Ferguson and Jack Bancroft? I know we were going to limit info to just Mozley, but if they are with us, we can keep an eye on them and check their reactions and they'll have the credibility of their organizations." Richard turned from the window. "Mitchell is coming back."

As soon as he entered, Mitchell scanned the room and everything seemed in order. "Thanks, Guys, I really appreciated the break. You understand I wouldn't have left you here alone except I got word you have some high connections and were a-okay." He grinned.

"I'm sure you wouldn't and we are truly flattered that we have such good credentials. I'm afraid this is a rather barren place. You were right, the army did scour the premises." Chloe smiled. "Did you get enough to eat?"

"Oh, yes m'am." He put the hefty grocery bag on the table. "I can camp out here now for at least two days!"

"Good, We'll be going. Take care in this neighborhood. It's rather dangerous." Chloe paused at the door.

"Oh, I will. Dad always said 'most danger is right outside your door.' The thing that bothers me is how quiet this place is. I mean most apartment buildings are noisy. People talking and swearing and all. I think this guy was the only one who lived here. I'm sure glad that guy had a clock. Nice to hear the ticking."

Richard noticed he'd left the clock door open and casually walked over to close it unobserved. As soon as the door shut, he heard a metallic thud. "Ticking! My God it's different! Quick everybody out! Now!" John grabbed Chloe and Mitchell by the arms and pushed them down the hall. John was in hot pursuit. Richard kept shoving them across the street. "Run, don't stop!" They paused for breath half way down the block and looked back just as an explosion rocked the building they had left, sending a huge fireball into the air.

CHAPTER SIX

The street was crawling with army jeeps, police cars, fire trucks and ambulances. Chloe wiped a shaking hand over her soot-covered forehead. "Well, that was close!"

Mitchell left a group of army men and came over to them. "Wow, Sir. That was exciting. How did you know?"

Richard smiled at him, "The clock ticking. I grew up in a house with clocks. My Mother had a clock in every room in the house. Each has its own sound. The ticking of that clock had changed from what it was when we first got there and all at once it was very irregular. I just thought there was no reason and we'd better scram." He didn't mention investigating the clock, removing contents or closing the door.

"Gee! This is one I can tell my guys back at the barracks." Mitchell hesitated, "Thank you, Sir. I think you saved my life." He hesitated as if to say more, then turned and walked back to his group.

"I think when you closed the door, you triggered a remote device. The firemen say the explosives were in the basement. One interesting bit of info, no one else was in the building. This is a really big enterprise. They, whoever they are, had this whole building for that one guy and his book was so important, they blew up the building to protect it or themselves. They don't want anything to point back to them. We're talking super planning and big money here." John leaned against a car hood behind him. "What do you say we take a closer look at that book?"

"Good idea. Let's clean up and then meet at the HSD office. Meanwhile, I'll get in touch with Jo, Jack and Mozley and set up our little trek to Chicago. I'm also going to get in touch with the governor of Illinois and the mayor of Chicago. We're going to need some local and state police help, but we have to keep everything quiet, no need starting a panic. I'll ask then to have any forces in civilian clothes." Richard turned as he spoke. "Can you drive Chloe home, John? I'll meet you there in about an hour."

"Right, we'll be ready." As he headed for the car and Richard for the nearest army jeep, John grinned at Chloe, "Do you think that clock was not really an antique and the owner is an antique dealer who just didn't want to be found out?"

"John, John, what are we going to do with you? Do be serious!"

"Can you hear me, Richard?" Don Mozley was screaming at the top of his voice, trying to drown out the sound of the helicopter blades.

"Loud and clear. Thanks for getting this army chopper for us, especially one that can hold six passengers. Is everyone buckled in? We're going to Fort Sheridan outside Chicago. Relax and enjoy the ride. I'll fill you all in later." Richard leaned back in his seat and watched the ground recede beneath him. Luckily it was a warm fall day. The hour and forty-minute ride in the small jet from Washington to Toledo had been uneventful. *Thank God*, Richard thought. *We've had enough excitement for one day*.

"I still don't understand why we can't fly into Chicago. Why did we have to go first to Toledo, for God's sake? Are you trying to hide our destination?" Don screamed back.

"Tell you later," Richard pointed to the pilot and turned back to look out the window.

Within ninety minutes, the helicopter had landed. Everyone got out and boarded an army SUV that was <u>not</u> marked 'U.S. Army'. Do you want me to stay here, Sir? The pilot asked.

"Yes, please. I don't know when we'll be returning. Do you have a cell phone so I can call about departure time?"

"Sure here's my card. I'll be gone for the next hour. Looking up some food, but I'll have my cell phone with me." He waved them off.

"I'll drive. I think I know the general route." Richard climbed into the driver's seat and Mozley and Jo got in front beside him. The rest piled in the back.

"Well, that was something. I didn't know Fort Sheridan was still an army installation. Thought they closed it in '93." Don looked at the luxury homes all around them.

"It's not an army installation as such. All operations were stopped, but the army retained two parcels of about 114 acres for Army Reserve missions. They sold 185 acres to the Navy for military housing and offices. Of the 415 acres left some is National Historic Landmark District and some has been sold to a Local Redevelopment Authority for up-scale housing. I thought if we landed here it would be harder to trail us and we can get back to the helicopter and take off at will and not wait for airport clearance. I left information for everyone that we would be leaving tomorrow. This might make whoever is doing all this think that they have an extra day.

"This is a good chance to fill you all in on what's coming down. We've found, thanks to Dudley, that some weapons armed with chemicals are missing: one land mine, two M2 mortars and four M55 rockets."

Jo and Jack spoke at once, "You're not serious! You're kidding!"

"I wish I were. They found the land mine at Aberdeen and it has been safely secured. The man who had murdered to get the badge to get into the bunker, presumably to blow up the land mine, was apprehended. When we checked his apartment we found this lead to the Chicago connection we're after now. Don't know which of the lost munitions this will be. We've got about an hour and a half ride south to 47th street."

"Do you mean to tell me the army has not only muffed its serial number tracking but lost some chemical weapons?" Jo asked. "That stupid arrogant Dowell probably had something to do with it!"

Quietly, Jack asked, "Have you contacted the FBI or CIA about this? No one has contacted me. Anyone you, Jo?" Jo shook her head. "So why were we kept in the dark?"

"Dudley found out about the missing munitions. The army hasn't noticed it yet. So we kept it secret." Richard answered.

Quieter still, Jack persisted, "Does everyone on the committee know about this?"

"We have operated on the need to know basis. We told Mozley so we could get into Dudley's office and now you two since we might need backup."

"So Beel, Dowell and Andrews are still out of the ring?"

"Right!" Richard nodded.

"I don't like this one bit! What you're saying is that you don't trust us." Jack was raising his voice.

"Would you in my shoes, Jack? Dudley was murdered by someone using VX. Another someone with enough pull had so doctored the lists of weapons that no one except a real nut with a phobia for lists, someone like Dudley, found out about it. Maybe they were counting on his finding missing weapons. That elusive someone with connections to this committee may have set him up." Richard stared at him in the rear view mirror.

Sullenly, Jack asked, "What else did you find in the apartment in D.C.?

Richard glanced back at Chloe and John, then answered, "We found a scrap of paper with the name Tabor Rester, a Chicago address, with this Friday's date on it. We also found a telephone book with Armad Beel's name in it along with another name, Louise Wiggins. Any of those names ring a bell?"

"Yes," Jo responded, "I met Louise at a party. She was Armad's date, really gorgeous, an exotic-type look, jet black hair and eyes, born in Indiana, mother from India and dad British, an engineer. I think she had a hard time growing up; the kids called her a half-breed. She works for DOD now, very responsible job. I think she shares an apartment with Armad sometimes. It's sort of an on again off again relationship."

"You found all that out at a party?" Chloe was incredulous.

"People talk to Jo. MOST people trust her!" Jack scowled at Richard.

"I think she'd had too much to drink and something was bothering her, but she didn't say what. She is one smart cookie, very much the controlling type. She definitely doesn't like men." Jo ignored Jack's sarcasm.

"Okay, we're now going south on 41, people, help me look for 94 East. It'll be going south but it's marked east. Jo, in the glove compartment is a picture of Rester. Do you want to hand it around? He's 45 years old, has a wife and two grown children, dropped out of high school, and works at a garage repairing trucks, good with mechanical things."

There's 94 East!" John called.

"Okay, now we follow this, go though the loop and on to 43rd street. There are a lot of one-way streets, after that to get to 47th, so we'll have to feel our way from there."

"So you think the mixed-up serial numbers is a cover-up for the stolen munitions?" Jack asked.

"Funny you should put it that way, Jack. With my inverse thinking, I'm just beginning to wonder if it's the other way around: the stolen munitions are a diversion for the mixed-up serial number. The thinking seems to be that a lot of money and a great deal of upper level planning has gone into this munitions theft. Mini gangsters don't challenge the U.S. Army. So far, the land mine was bungled, which would be inconsistent with the level of planning. By the way, don't get huffy about Richard suspecting you, Jack. He suspects me, too, and I've known him since you were in grade school." Mozley spoke for the first time since they had started.

"I didn't know you were as old as Richard!" Jo exclaimed.

Jack shouted, "Touché!" and Mozley exclaimed, "Bless you, my child!" Richard just chuckled, but the drive had become less tense.

The stores in the loop were open and the "L" was thundering away overhead as they passed underneath and continued on 94 East.

When they could hear each other again, Richard commented, "The note marked the date as this Friday for something, God knows what, to happen. But they may have upped their schedule a bit."

Mozley continued from there. "Richard didn't mention that he, Chloe, and John got out of that apartment minutes before it blew up. This may have alerted those who set the bomb that they were on to the next move. It's like chess isn't it?"

"So, if they got the land mine, then the mortars and rockets are left to find. Right? What size and weight are the things we're looking for?" Jo asked.

"They made the M55 Rockets in the 50's to deliver toxic chemicals on large areas at some distance. The rocket has a warhead, that's where the chemical agent is, and then an aluminum nozzle with spring loaded fins and a rocket motor. You can recognize the rocket by the three green bands around the body. It's 83 inches long and can carry about 10 pounds of either mustard or VX agent. The warhead's 57 pounds, the propellant weighs about 20 pounds; I don't know the weight of the rocket or rounds. The rockets are generally stored with about fifteen rounds per pallet. I looked this up last night." Richard was following a slow moving SUV that speeded up every time he tried to pass.

"If it's 83 inches long, you wouldn't just walk around with it. What about the mortars?" Jo persisted.

"The 4.2inch M2 mortar is not exactly small, although the army describes it as 'mobile'. It weighs 640 pounds and can be broken down into six major parts the largest weighing about 162 pounds. It could be towed in a light handcart. It's fired from the ground and is accurate within 4000 yards."

"My God, that's over two miles!" Jo gasped.

"I'm going to turn left, is that right? Follow me on this map. On 43rd now and I'm just following the one-way signs to get to 47th. The odd numbers should be on the right." Richard had slowed to a crawl, much to the consternation of the drivers behind him

"This is not the neighborhood to make enemies in automobiles, Richard," Mozley warned. "There it is! Uh oh! I don't like the looks of this. See the quarter-ton truck parked across the street with the quarter-ton trailer. The trailer is covered with heavy canvas. These babies are a good size and in a civilian neighborhood. We'll have to be careful here. We're working for the federal government and have no jurisdiction in Chicago or Illinois."

"I called both the governor and mayor. Back-up should be around here but undercover. We won't recognize them. What do you suggest?" Richard asked.

"I have my cell phone," Jo said. "I'll call the office and get them to issue a search warrant. Don't worry, we have a code so an intercepted call cannot be understood."

"Yes, but we can't go to pick up the warrant. I hate to leave this place and no cabs venture around here to take you. Wouldn't trust them if they did." Don answered. "Any way, with the Patriots Act or for that matter even without it, I don't think we'll need a warrant to retrieve army munitions. Wait, someone's coming out."

"Four men are walking this way. See, one is like the picture Jo just passed around. It's Rester. He's getting in the cab of the truck and the short Mexican-looking guy is going to drive. The other two are getting in that '97 Taurus right behind them." A tall blond fellow with muscles to match his stride and a hefty black man wearing a red bandana around his head, started the Taurus motor. "So what do we do now?" Jack asked.

"Better get them now! If they get on the highway and we lose them we're in deep trouble. Somebody get the licenses just in case." Richard growled as he sung around and blocked the truck's movement.

"Are you crazy? We don't have any authority!" Jack sputtered. When the men in the Taurus saw what was happening, they quickly backed up, made a cramped u-turn and took off. Two seemingly empty cars, immediately came to life and blocked their exit. Richard could see the men driving the cars that blocked the Taurus were not in uniform. The truck was so hemmed in, it couldn't move.

For a split second, no sound was made, and then from the Taurus the ratting of a machine gun broke the eerie silence. "Damn, we want them alive for information! We're in big trouble if they shoot the trailer and it has CW's in it." Richard exclaimed. He jumped out of the car and started running, head down, for the truck. Returning gunshots sounded from inside the cars blocking the Taurus. Two men, huddled beside the car, were also shooting at the Taurus.

As soon as Richard exited, Jack jumped out the back of the SUV and Jo from the front and both circled the other side of the truck opposite from where Richard was heading. John had quickly and quietly followed Richard. No sound came from the Taurus. Jack reached the driver's side of the truck first and yanked open the door. He pulled the trembling Mexican from the driver's seat. Jo stood beside him. Rester in the front seat of the truck was diverted from Richard's approach, and leaned over the steering wheel, gun in hand aimed at Jo. She froze looking down the barrel of the gun. Jack glanced up at that moment and threw himself between Jo and the gun just as Richard grabbed Rester's hand and the gun exploded.

Of a sudden, several parked cars came to life and men poured forth. One of the men handcuffed the Mexican and leaned him against the truck to search. Two more ran up shouting, "The guys in the Taurus are goners!"

Rester wrangled through to the driver's side, shaking off Richard's hold. He grabbed Jo by the neck and pointed his gun at her head. "One move and you're dead!" he shouted. Everyone froze. Pushing her before him, he started toward the SUV and motioned to Don in the front seat. "Out!"

Quietly Don scooted from the seat. Rester pushed Jo into the driver's seat and got in beside her. "Now, my Dear, just start the motor and we will leave this little group." He didn't see Chloe huddled in the back seat. As soon as Jo started the engine, Chloe sprang up, struck Rester's hand holding the gun with her left hand in a karate chop as she brought the butt of her gun down on his skull. The crack of gun butt on bone echoed in the car. Rester slumped to the floor.

As Richard ran to the door, Chloe called out. "I didn't want to shoot him. I think we can still question the man. Are you okay, Jo?"

Quietly, Jo answered, "Yes, where's Jack?"

Richard was bending over Jack slumped on the road. "Quick call an ambulance!"

One of the men from the come-alive cars walked up to him. "I already have, Sir. I'm Lieutenant Durkin from the State Police, tactical squad agent. The governor called us and we've been waiting for you. I'm afraid the two in the Taurus are dead. We had no choice. Our little Mexican friend is very much alive and eager to be helpful in return for not being turned in to the authorities. I think he's an illegal immigrant."

Richard went to the truck and loosened the canvas cover. The men watching caught their breath. Two 4.2" M2 mortars complete with shells and firing equipment stared back at them. Immediately Richard returned the cover.

"Senor. I help. They make me load guns. I no want to." The Mexican, with large fearful eyes, called out.

"I'm sure you didn't. Could you tell us where they were taking these guns?" Richard kept his voice steady as he walked over to the man.

"We go to the West 14th and Canal Street. There is a vacant lot there near the railroads. We are to park..k..k and be ready for tomorrrrow morning. I no know the target! Believe me..e..e!" he stuttered in his anxiety to be helpful.

Richard pulled out the map of Chicago from the SUV and opened it on the hood of the car. "Well, if these guns have a 4000 yard range it should be anything within a circle drawn from 14th and Canal as it's center. My guess would be the Union station and the Sears Tower early in the morning when they are the busiest."

"Good, Lord, Sir. We're talking thousands of people!" Durkin's face paled.

Richard had forgotten the plain-clothed men around him and grimaced that he had unwittingly disclosed the target and information. But he had no choice; he'd have to include them in the procedures. Time was running out. "If those mortars are loaded with chemicals, Lieutenant, it would be at least that many. We'll have to have an armed guard to see that those mortars get back to the army base at Rock Island. Keep this very quiet. No press! Can you handle this?"

"Yes, Sir." Durkin turned to four men who had been standing out of earshot. "Men, we have to get this truck and trailer down to Rock Island Arsenal ASAP. Kenny, you drive and take Walkins with you. I'll be in touch with the Commander to tell you what to do with it when you get there. At no time let it out of your sight, to go to the john or eat. In fact, just don't leave the truck. Bill, you and Sam ride shotgun in a car behind them."

"Lieutenant, could you see about removing these bodies in the car? Richard asked.

"Two of my men are already removing them, Sir. We'll take the men to the morgue and await further orders. One lucky thing about this location is that shoot-outs are not uncommon!"

An ambulance came screaming down the street. Three EMT's jumped out and ran to Jack. The fellow bending over Jack called back to Richard, "He's been shot in the chest and it looks like it's near his lungs. He's losing a lot of blood. We'll have to take him in right away, as soon as we get him some oxygen, saline IV and sugar. Sam's tryin' to stop the bleeding now." The other man brought out a stretcher.

"I'll go with him, Richard. It's the least I can do. He saved my life." Jo whispered as she followed the stretcher to the ambulance. As the ambulance driver tried to divert her, she screamed, "What do you mean I can't ride back there?" Then Jo shouted to the men as she flashed her badge and climbed aboard. "I'm FBI! Now move it!"

A second ambulance coming in passed them. The attendants jumped out and headed for Rester. "This man is in police custody. Could you see that he is given over to the Rock Island Army Base Hospital?" Richard asked as the two men bent over him.

"No problem. But it will cost the army a lot to take an ambulance that far out of town." One of the men commented.

"His name is Rester. Be careful if he comes to, he's dangerous. The commander will be expecting him. Don will you sign papers for them?"

"Yeah and I'll ride along with him," Don volunteered. "Just to keep an eye on him or in case he wakes up and wants to play checkers!"

Richard turned a tired face toward Chloe and John. "John, could you bring the Mexican with us. As of now he's the only one we've got whom we can question. We still have to locate where those two mortars were suppose to land. As soon as we do, I'll call the governor."

Quietly Chloe commented, "That leaves four M55 rockets. The deadliest of the bunch! And they are out there somewhere in the U.S."

CHAPTER SEVEN

"First you stand me up for dinner when you are in Aberdeen, Maryland, then you hotfoot off to Chicago. I thought at first you had decided you were not the marrying type." Harriet smiled up at Richard as they stood near the receiving gate at the Dulles airport waiting for the plane from France to bring Rene and Gabriel.

"How could you possibly believe that…" Richard turned to her in disbelief.

"My Dear, I'm teasing. My, you really are wound up and tense. Is it the chemical weapon's business or is it seeing Gabriel?" Harriet studied his face closely.

"Look. I am sorry, there is just so much going on. A little of both I guess. The weapons thing is coming to a head. It's become more complex than anything we've done to date. Then, this is the first time I've seen Gabriel since that rescue from her kidnappers in London. Guess I don't know what to expect." He smiled self-conscinously.

"Fine. Let's talk about one thing at a time. What have you found out about the missing chemicals, and don't give me the 'this is top secret thing'. If I'm going to be a widow someday I want to know why!" She took his arm and squeezed his hand.

"Well, to begin with, we got the stolen mortars in Chicago before they were fired. From what we can gather from the Mexican who was forced to drive the truck, they were headed for a vacant parking lot within range of both the Sears Tower and Union Station. Rester, the guy in charge of this little escapade is still unconscious from a cracked skull that Chloe gave him. We're still trying to find the location of the M55 rockets."

"My, my, Chloe cracks skulls! Who would have thought? I suppose this is stupid to ask, but was there a gun fight?" Only the clenching and unclenching of her fingers gave any indication her light tone was hiding a more nervous response.

"Well, yes, sort of." He grinned.

"Oh, dear, and I missed all the fun." She kept her tone light. "So, where do you go next?"

Changing the subject, he replied, "Unless I'm mistaken, I go down the aisle tomorrow and make you Mrs. Richard Moore." Then he turned serious. "I really feel bad that I've done so little on the preparations. Just, everything is happening so fast! We should have at least a year to plan and savor all this. At least that's what all the books say. When do your folks come? Where are they staying? How many and who are they? I can't believe I know so little about you!"

"Ah ha, a mystery woman from Iowa! Now that's an oxymoron if ever I heard one. Well, my one disappointment is that Mom and Dad are dead and they won't be at my wedding. But my sister from Chicago and one from Texas are coming with their husbands and several college friends who live in Delaware, Massachusetts, and Colorado with their husbands, then people I know from CDC and I got a list of your friends from John. I can't believe so many can come at such short notice. Chloe and John have been incredible. Chloe has reserved rooms for everyone from out of town at the Cosmos Club and arranged for a caterer for a reception after the ceremony, at your house in Potomac, it's her wedding gift. John reserved the church plus organist and has selected the restaurant and planned the rehearsal dinner tonight. So you see there is very little for me to do. Which is lucky, because at work I'm just finally getting that Smithwick Lab so it can operate on it's own and I can return to the CDC." She stopped to catch her breath and smiled, "I did take time to get a gorgeous wedding dress and nightgown!"

"Obviously the most important thing to do!" Richard laughed and felt better than he had in weeks.

"I hope I've invited the right friends for you. John gave me a list of those you work with and Chloe added a few, she said she's checked with you." She frowned, "I hope I didn't omit any! Everything has moved so quickly. Chloe said there are two times when you make enemies in your family: one is when you omit inviting some first cousin to your wedding and second is when you have children and you don't give them the names the family thinks you should."

They were so engrossed in each other they had not noticed that the plane from Paris had landed and people were filing out of the gate.

"There he is! 'Ello, Richard." Rene called walking up to them. He was pushing a cart laden with luggage.

Harriet saw a tall young women, with raven hair, brilliant blue eyes and the grace of a cat artfully push past Rene and stand before Richard. She dramatically threw her arms around him and brought her face close to his. Gabriel lightly kissed him on both cheeks, then stood back and looked closely, searching his face. Rene broke the awkward pause, "Let the poor man breath, Gabriel!" He turned to Harriet, "And introduce us to this enchanting woman, Richard."

Flustered, Richard turned to Harriet, "Rene, Gabriel, I'd like you to know my fiancée, Harriet Hobbs soon to be Harriet Moore."

"My dear, I am so happy to know you. Richard is a lucky man." Rene took her hand in both his and his smile was sincere and warm.

"I am so happy for you both." Gabriel continued to stare at Richard. "You are very fortunate, Miss Hobbs, Richard is a wonderful man and has been like a father to me." Her voice turned frosty as she intoned 'father.' The blue eyes turned to blue ice. She looked first at Harriet and then back to Richard. The glance lasted only a moment before she smiled, but for that one instant, the hatred was so startlingly vivid, Harriet caught her breath. *She knows*, Harriet thought. *Someone told her.* She glanced at Rene. *From the look on*

Rene's face, he was the one who told her. He knows Richard's little secret, too. Oh dear! Poor Richard!

Mercifully, John broke the strained, uncomfortable silence as he ran up to them, shouting, "Damn! The traffic was unbelievable! I knew you'd beat me here! Rene! Gabriel! Welcome! You got my e-mail! The guest rooms are ready and waiting! I see you've met the woman who has old Richard here spinning and ready to walk down the aisle, a tethered man if ever I saw one and damn lucky at that!" He paused for breath, shook Rene's hand and bussed Gabriel on the cheek. Three of the four looked at him gratefully.

Gabriel viewed him as a hunter does a doomed deer and spoke sweetly, "My hero. Bless you for giving us a place where we can put our heads. I've missed you." She gave him a hug.

"Yes, we have met the lovely Miss Hobbs, soon to be Mrs. Moore. Indeed, Richard is lucky. We can't wait to know her better, but all the excitement, invigorating as it may be, at my age, I need to rest and catch my breath. " Rene looked tired and drawn.

"My chariot awaits. You don't mind do you, Richard, if I whisk Rene and the lovely Gabriel off to my lair where they can freshen up for the rehearsal dinner this evening? This will give you two time to be alone for a while." John glanced at Richard and Harriet. "These last few days have been filled for Richard…" he paused, afraid he might go too far, then hastened on. "And Harriet. But being the clever chap and best man that I am, I have everything under control for tonight. You will love the food, Rene, an honest to God French chef! Let's go! Good Lord, is all this luggage yours? How long did it take you to get through customs?"

"I'm afraid I pulled diplomatic privilege and we were whisked through all the inspecting. A very kind young man put our stuff on a cart, so we are ready to go. I might add only one of these cases is mine. Gabriel, like her mother, travels in style!" Rene laughed as he pointed to the cart.

Gabriel took John's arm, "I wanted to look my best for you. I don't want any American out-dressing me. I want all your attention!"

John was pleased, "Okay let's go!" He waved to Richard and Harriet. "See you tonight, eight sharp, black tie, instructions are on your e-mail." He waved gaily as he squeezed Gabriel's arm and propelled her away.

Rene looked uncomfortable. He smiled, "The young, so impulsive, so wrapped up in themselves. We will have time later to talk...so much to catch up on. I'd best hurry or they will leave without me. My dear," he turned once more to Harriet, "Richard is a fine man. I wish you both well." He patted Richard on the shoulder and turned to follow the cart burdened with luggage.

Into the flat silence, Richard whispered, "Well, that went well, better then I had expected."

Harriet stared at Richard in disbelief. She thought, *you're didn't notice all that was happening. You really think everything is just fine. How naive you are, how sweet, and what a remarkable man Rene is! You have caused him so much pain, but Rene seems so forgiving, so concerned. Should I explain to you what just happened? That Gabriel is strung tighter than a top, obviously hoping for revenge through John? No, better you go on as is. You have enough on your mind.* Aloud she said, "Yes, now, do you have a black tie get-up or do we go shopping?"

"Thank you, John, everything has gone so smoothly. The food was truly a delight. No rehearsal dinner has ever been so well planned and executed. You could go into business as a caterer!" Richard was feeling relieved, mellow, magnanimous and full of both food and wine as he glanced around the room.

"Afraid I can't take credit for all of this. Chloe put me in contact with her friend, Adele Comstock, who took over finding the right chef, planning the menu, even came by this afternoon to double check on the flowers. Seems she knows everyone in Washington and set up a party here for Chloe just this past year. Doesn't Gabriel look ravishing? I must admit, I've been flattered with her attention." John spotted Gabriel across the room and their eyes met. She threw him a kiss. "I know she's young and so vulnerable, so open and spontaneous, not like most of the women I've known. Strange, she makes me feel young and vital."

"Well, look here. You're not exactly in your dotage you know!" Richard laughed.

Harriet walked up just in time to hear the last part of the conversation. She appraised Gabriel in a clinging, low cut black gown laughing too loudly at an elderly man's story and wondered if she and John were looking at the same person. *I've seen black widows who looked less harmless*, she thought. Rene's approach smothered a comment on the end of her tongue.

"Lovely dinner, Richard. A truly remarkable chef! Harriet, my dear, you look stunning. All ready for the big day?"

"Yes, thank you. If I can keep Richard's mind off work long enough to walk down the aisle." She smiled. Rene was not at all what she had expected. *He's so kind and yet worldly*, she thought.

Instantly a look of apprehension crossed Rene's face. "Work? Surely no work could interfere with such an important day, unless of course it was something very serious, " he laughed and said half seriously, "something of a national crisis."

Immediately, Richard cut in, "The only work I'm really worried about is that I haven't had time to work at getting to know Harriet's family. If you'll excuse us, I think I should do that now. I see your sisters have finished dessert and I'll have a chance to find out all the things they know about you that you haven't told me." He took Harriet's arm and firmly led her away.

When they were out of earshot of Rene he said in a low, controlled voice, "Please don't ever refer to my work again to Rene. He, of all people, knows what I do. While I can trust him, just a hint from his change of manner and perhaps a waiter or a bus boy will mention something to someone else. Plus, he has many connections. Please be more careful."

His tone of voice as well as his words and the biting pressure of his fingers on her arm took Harriet aback. She raised her head, disengaged her arm from his and spoke firmly, "What are you saying? I am not a child. I do not have to be cautioned on what to say. Honestly, Richard, you are becoming paranoid and it's not humorous anymore."

"Look, you have no idea what's going on here or the gravity. All I ask is you don't refer to my work!" He had raised his voice.

She had no time to respond as they were now standing before her two older sisters and she forced a smile and motioned to the smaller of the women. "Richard, Helen here was four when I was born and Hannah was two." She turned to the two ladies standing before them. "I think he wants to know something wicked about me that only you two could dredge up. Something he can blackmail me with and force me to cook dinners or make beds, load that barge, etc." She forced a laugh.

Helen, a small brunette with a heart shaped face, looked quickly up. Something in Harriet's face bothered her, but she smiled, "What would you like to know? Maybe about the time I talked her into smoking cigarettes behind the garage and Dad found us? Or the time she ate a whole can of beets….."

"Oh no, not that!" Harriet began to laugh more genuinely this time.

"How about, why all your names start with 'H'? Does your family have an alphabet thing?" Richard was loosing his tense look.

Hannah was tall and dark, almost as tall as Richard himself. She had taken a sudden dislike to her sister's intended, she had noted the sharp exchange, but then she took dislikes to most things quite easily. "Helen was named Helen Howard, after a nurse who was killed in World War II. Our mother was a nurse, too and was best friends with Ms Howard. I was named for my grandmother."

Harriet laughed, "And I was named for my father's cousin who was supposed to be very wealthy and would leave me all her money. Unfortunately, she lost everything in the depression!"

John came up hurriedly and interrupted, "Sorry, Richard, but could I see you for a minute? Excuse us, ladies. I'll bring him right back."

As soon as they left the room, Richard turned to John, "What's up?"

"Step in here." John pointed to a small room off the hall.

Don Mozley and Chloe were waiting. "I just got back from Rock Island Arsenal and I brought Rester back with me in an army jet." Don explained. "I've put him in Walter Reed Hospital under guard. Rester comes and goes into consciousness, has periods of stability and wants to talk. I think he's hoping to get off light if he cooperates.

It's kind of hard to make sense of what he's saying, keeps going in and out of sleep. Something about Tooele, Utah and he mentioned, I think he was trying to say Dowell. I checked with Green and Dowell has been out at Tooele a good deal lately. What do you think?"

"If our surmise is correct and this is a diversion action, then we should be able to eliminate Aberdeen and Tooele from the main event. We must begin concentrating on the other sites as the primary action. However, every diversion turns out to have a danger built in so Tooele must be the next diversion. Good Lord, what must the main event be if the diversions would have been so devastating?" Chloe shook her head.

"One other thing, Rester keeps talking about the second week in November. That means we have a little time to try and figure all this out." Mozley lowered himself into an easy chair and rubbed his forehead. "I tell you I'm plain tuckered out."

"How would it be if one of us goes to Tooele to try and find out about the last smoke-screen tactic? I'd like to see someone go to Newport, Indiana, too. For some reason, that's the one site every one in this committee has been avoiding visiting. Why? Why draw our attention to every other place? Also, we need to find out exactly who has visited what site and when. Plus, that construction and oil delivery company that the guy they caught at Aberdeen worked for. Does that company serve any of the other sites? There is one other thing that has bothered me. We hear nothing about Andrews. Why? Why is everyone else involved in something suspicious and Andrews so quiet? He didn't even attend that first meeting at the HSC Building. I know you said he had to take care of some terrorist threat, Don, and you'd brief him. Was there such a scare? Did you brief him?" Richard stared at Don.

"I went to his office and talked. Thought the subject too delicate for a memo. I can check about the threat Andrews used as an excuse. Is there any rehearsal dinner left? Just got back from Chicago. I'm not dressed but I could eat in the kitchen." Don all but rubbed his stomach.

"My dear boy, how thoughtless we are. Of course you can eat, and with me in the main dining room. I'll have them fix you a plate." Chloe extended her hand. "As for you, Richard, I take it the wedding will go on as scheduled. I'll start the check on the oil deliveries, who traveled where, when and ask more closely after Andrews. You must get back to your fiancée. Doesn't Gabriel look lovely? I know you think so, John."

"Indeed I do. We had planned to do the town after the dinner, but I can do checks this evening for you if you want." John rose, also.

"No thanks. I'm going to feed Don. Then I'll call an old friend and do my own snooping. He can get more information than any organization I know of and in a shorter time. If we have until November, then you can enjoy your wedding night, Richard, but that's going to be about all the free time you'll have."

"Damn, just what I need. Harriet and I had a little tiff just now. She will think me a real bore to leave her right after dinner, but I'm unusually concerned about this case. So many more people are involved than our regular work. Plus we are acting on suppositions, not facts. We only know what's going to happen when it almost happens. Also, for some reason, I am worried about Harriet's safety. Just new husband jitters, I guess, a new feeling of responsibility." Richard smiled sheepishly.

Chloe paused halfway to the door, half-supporting a sleepy Don. "Strange you should say that. For the first time since I've been working with the Noir, I feel very uneasy, also."

CHAPTER EIGHT

Nestled deep in down pillows, Gabriel surveyed the room, a very pleasant decor with a small sitting area and a lit fireplace to dispense the slight fall chill. *This will do nicely*, she thought. *Yes, I can see marrying John would do very well. I can continue to live like a princess and give Richard and Harriet a difficult time all at once.* She smiled smugly. *John was very attentive last night, showing me all the nightspots. It wasn't Paris, but I can always go back for a visit when I want.*

A light, knock at the door disturbed her reverie. She glanced in the mirror on her bedside table to check her hair and make-up and then cooed, "Come in?"

Rene peeked around the door. "My, dear, you should ask who it is before you invite me in," he chided.

"Oh, Papa, you are so old fashioned, dear but old-fashioned. Did you sleep well?"

"Like the dead. I'm still recovering from that magnificent dinner last evening. Just thought I'd poke my head in to see how you slept. What will you be wearing to the wedding and when will you be ready to leave?" He seated himself in the chintz-covered chair by the bed.

"Papa, I have a frightful headache. We got in so late last night. I thought just perhaps I could be excused from the wedding and maybe feel well enough to go to the reception." She put her hand to her forehead.

"Mais certainment, no! This is not a tea party! This is Richard's wedding! The most important day in a man's life! If you are in a coma, you are excused, otherwise we go, both of us!"

"You of all people should not have to go to see this man's happiness!" She flung back the covers, jumped out and flounced over to the dresser. Picking up her hairbrush, she began brushing her hair vigorously.

"Ma Cherie. What is done is done and over. We must move on…" his voice droned on.

Gabriel was not paying attention. Her eyes had moved to her jewelry box and lighted on a brooch, her mother's brooch, two hearts in silver entwined with ruby roses. Instantly a plan began to evolve in her mind. What if… She put down the brush, came to her father and kissed him on the head. "You are right, Papa. I overreacted. I just feel so badly for you. I shall put on my dress, and a smile and go with you. When should we leave?"

Rene viewed her suspiciously. She had given in too easily. What was she scheming? "John is to drive us and your Grandmother to the church. The ceremony is at four. John said driving time is forty minutes. We should be ready to leave around three. The reception is at Richard's house on the Potomac. What are you planning? You reconcile too easily just now. You have never done the dramatic. I feel uneasy with you. Don't do the dramatic now!" He stood and came over to her.

Gabriel smiled serenely. "Honestly, Papa, first you worry that I won't go and now that I'll go and scream or something. Give me some credit. I promise to behave. Now will you go have breakfast and let me choose a dress and get ready?" She hugged him and shoved him toward the door.

Rene left but hesitated outside the door. Purposefully he walked down the hall and paused outside Chloe's room, then rapped softly on the door.

"Come," called Chloe.

He paused at the door, "Do you have a moment?"

"Yes, of course." Chloe was sitting fully dressed, a cup of tea on the table by her fireside, the morning paper in her hand.

"Forgive the intrusion but could we talk a few minutes?"

Chloe motioned to a chair facing her. "Yes, of course. Do have a chair. Would you like some tea?"

"No, thank you. I've breakfasted. I hesitated to impose on you. I was reading and heard you come in quite late last night, later than Gabriel even. I am not questioning you, just explaining why I would understand if you were too tired to talk." He glanced around her room. "What a lovely house this is, a fireplace in each large and comfortable bedroom, a very accommodating Mrs. Adams to take care of every need. Young John lives well."

"Yes, indeed, as we all do. I take it you approve of his attentions to Gabriel?" Chloe surveyed him closely.

"It is about Gabriel I want to consult you. You see," he hesitated, "I don't know exactly where to begin..."

"As a not too often quoted American president once said 'always begin at the beginning.'" Chloe smiled quietly at him.

"Well, before we came to the United States, it came to my attention that Gabriel had an" he hesitated for the right word, "unusual attachment to Richard, an unhealthy attachment. I felt she should know of her real father's identity, so I told her." Chloe caught her breath and her teacup clattered as she sat it down hurriedly. In a woman of lesser self-control, the reaction would have been much more pronounced. Rene raised his eyes to hers, "Yes, I knew of Marie and Richard when I saw Gabriel growing up. Her heritage should be obvious to anyone with half an eye. I chose to ignore it when I saw Marie's resemblance in Gabriel as she grew older. But now, I worry. When I told her of her biological father, Gabriel became angry and then just as quickly, she became docile. This is not like her. Again, just now, first she didn't want to go to the wedding ceremony and then just as quickly agreed. It is as if she were planning something. I feel uneasy."

Chloe sat silently digesting what she had heard. Finally she broke the silence, "As well you might! I agree completely. What should we do?"

"I thought you might suggest something." Rene sat forward in his chair.

Chloe thought out loud, "Obviously she is planning something. You know her better than I since I was not allowed to communicate with her during her growing years. Would she plan something dramatic? Is that her style?"

Rene looked down at his hands and said quietly, "You must forgive me for keeping you away from her, but I had to blame someone or go crazy."

Chloe reached over and covered his folded hands with hers. "I understand, truly." She paused. "Would her reaction be dramatic or devious? What is her nature?"

"I would say devious. She is not a naturally mean person, just as Marie was not, but she has that sense of pride, of justice, hurting someone she feels has hurt her or her family. Probably getting even for any hurt she might imagine Richard had imposed on her mother or me. Does this make sense?" He studied Chloe's face.

"Perfect sense. I shall go in and talk with her. I'm glad you told me all this. We can possibly avert a tragedy, such as we were unable to do for Marie." She sighed. They both rose.

Rene squeezed the hands that he still held in his. "Thank you," he whispered.

"I will tell you what transpires," she promised.

After Rene had left, she walked to her dresser and studied her face in the mirror. Hooded, dark brown eyes stared back, eyes set in a firm, oval face surrounded by salt and pepper hair. But the eyes seemed tired, sleepy and tired. She smiled, *Rene is right. I did get back late last night, but it was worth it. I found out a great deal that will help Richard. But now I must help his daughter. I'm too old to be doing this*, she thought. Chloe rearranged the pearl choker at her throat as carefully as she changed her facial expression, went to the door and left the room.

"May I come in?" She had knocked and when she got no reply she'd opened the door a crack.

"Oh, Grandmamma, yes, do. I didn't hear you." Gabriel attempted to hide something she was doing.

Chloe stared at the package Gabreil had been trying to wrap and said, "Am I interrupting something."

"No…I…I was just wrapping a present for Harriet." She stammered and blushed.

"Why how lovely. What did you get her?"

"A silver brooch. I think she'll like it." Gabriel tried to push the package away.

"How considerate. May I see it?" Chloe came into the room.

If Gabriel had not been caught off guard she would have had an excuse, thought of a diversion, but being at a loss for words, she sullenly opened the box.

"Why, Gabriel, that was your mother's brooch! Are you sure you want to do this? I always come directly to the point. I do not play games, my dear. I think you know what would happen. Harriet would put this on, Richard would instantly recognize it and tell her, and you would spoil their wedding day for them both. Is that what you really want to do? What you don't know perhaps is that Richard gave that brooch to your mother. I would like to think you didn't know what would happen, but I'm afraid you did know and intended the results I have just mentioned." Chloe sat down on the bed and looked into Gabriel's eyes.

"You knew about them?" Gabriel barely mouthed the words.

"Yes, but too late to do anything about it. I'm hoping not to make that mistake again now. I strongly suggest you put the jewelry back in your box and we forget this ever happened. I realize you may not like me for saying this, but I love you and am willing to take the chance. Now show me what you are going to wear."

Gabriel, Chloe and Rene were seated in the front as the groom's family; John was the best man. The small church was packed. So many people to come on such short notice! Gabriel watched as Harriet came down the aisle in a filmy white dress with the late fall sunshine streaming though the church windows. Everything seemed to move in a slow motion trance. She saw the bride's auburn hair under the thinnest of lace veils, she heard Harriet's voice firmly answering the questions. Seated quietly between Rene and Chloe, wedged in as it were, she was motionless, but inside Gabriel was seething. She blocked out Richard's answers and instead heard her father's voice as he had said, "you have never done the dramatic." *Maybe I should*, she thought. *Maybe it's time I do the outrageous! The daring!* Of a sudden everything was over, all took place so quickly. But in that short time, Gabriel had made her resolve. She would find some way to change her image, some bold statement, something daring! With a frozen smile Gabriel waited on the church stairs and then in the car to the reception as John kept up an excited conversation. At the sight of Richard's house, Gabriel snapped out of her trance. *If Richard were not my father, I could be coming here as his bride* her thoughts a jumble of confusion.

John ushered her inside and brought drinks. Gabriel looked all around until she realized John had been talking to her and was waiting for an answer. "Hello, earth to Gabriel. I just said I want you to meet a colleague of mine. Well, actually we serve on the same committee so I guess that makes him a colleague. Armad Beel is a computer whiz and this is his date, Louise Wiggins."

Gabriel viewed the tall, exotic brunette and her rather nerdy companion with little interest. Both had a rather dark complexion, probably some oriental or Indian background. She smiled sweetly and asked of Louise. "What do you do? Are you on this committee, also?"

"I work in the DOD," Louise answered haughtily.

"Oh, come on now, tell them the exciting thing you do," Armad turned from Louise, "She's taken flying lessons. She and a group she knows are getting their pilot's licenses. She's learning on some old crop duster planes, she says, but still she will be able to fly just about anything."

Louise fixed him with a cold look. "Armad, I generally don't mention this. I'm sorry I ever told you. It's not very interesting."

John, whose gaze had been wandering instantly refocused at the word 'crop duster'. He scanned Louise more closely and then asked nonchalantly, "How long have you been doing this, Louise? Is it a large group you work with?"

"Not very long, just a few of us. Isn't this house gorgeous." Obviously wishing to change the subject, Louise looked about.

Gabriel ignored the attempt. If drama was what she wanted, this was it! "I'd love to learn to fly. May I join your group? Where do you meet? When? Oh I would love to try."

John looked uneasy. "Gabriel, would you be here in the States long enough to sign up for lessons?"

Gabriel ignored him. "Where do you fly?"

Armad answered for her, "They meet at a small field in Frederick, Virginia." He turned to Louise. "Didn't think I knew, did you? I saw the tag on your parachute yesterday.

If looks could kill, Armad would have been dead on the floor with his tongue hanging out. Louise was spared a response by the approach of a tall, distinguished gentleman, with what Gabriel called 'bedroom eyes'. He was graying at the temples but sprite of step and apparently had been listening to their conversation. He addressed John. "Hello, I'm Arnold Andrews. Understand you're on the same committee as Armad here." He nodded to Louise and Armad.

John seemed to become more alert, consciously blocking his view of Gabriel. "Glad to meet you. We were beginning to think there was no such person."

"Sorry I've missed your meetings. Been busy putting out fires." He spotted Gabriel, "Hi there."

Gabriel extended her hand. "Gabriel Beaumond. Louise was just telling us about her taking flying lessons and I'm trying to get her to let me join her group."

Andrews turned swiftly and gave Louise a piercing look, "Oh?"

"Really, it's not that exciting." The cool and sophisticated Louise suddenly looked flustered.

"Nonsense, I think it's great." Armad seemed bent on being helpful. To Gabriel he gushed, "Look, if you want to take lessons, I'll drive you out there. I'm sure now that I know it's in Frederick I can find it on my computer even if Louise here won't tell me."

"Now wait a minute. I've got all kinds of plans for Gabriel to go sightseeing. You'll have to get in line, Armad." John's good-natured scowl had a surprising edge.

Gabriel had made up her mind and John's interference just made her more determined. "Nonsense, we can still go sightseeing." She turned toward Armad. "I'm staying with my father at John's. Call me when you find the place and I'll be ready."

John picked up on the sharp look Andrews gave Louise. A voice behind him said, "Well, well, looks like if we can get the groom and Mozley over here, we could have a committee meeting!" Major Dowell joined the group. He eyed Gabriel, "And who's little angel might you be?"

Through gritted teeth, John introduced, "Gabriel Beaumond and her father are my guests this week. Major Dowell."

The Major took the hint. He leered at Louise instead. "They have an orchestra out in the garden. Do you dance as well as look lovely?" While Louise seemed to find the major repugnant, she also seemed eager to leave the conversation, so she took the proffered arm and departed.

Armad had the knack of once getting into a conversation of following it through as far as it would go. Plus, he had a fascination with things electrical and mechanical. "I can understand the interest you have in flying. Those days of strapping a 50-gallon tank of chemicals to a rickety old military plane that had been put out to pasture are gone. They have these really neat Ayers Turbo-Thrush and Air Tractor AT-400 Turbo Crop dusters now built just for that purpose. They have greater chemical capacity, too. The Air Turbo Thrush can take 2000 liters and the Air-tractor 802 can handle 3000 liters. And they have shorter take-offs and a lot faster spraying speeds.

"These planes have a four-hour flying time with a full payload, but you can fit them with a ferry kit that can turn the cargo hopper to a fuel tank and they can fly for twelve hours. Used to be they had spotters on the ground to tell the pilots where they had sprayed, but now the planes are equipped with Global Positioning System satellite technology so they know just where to go. Since Louise took up this flying bit, I've been looking up all the info on the Internet. I think the really exciting part is how low these planes can fly, about 1 to 2 meters above the ground. Golly, but I just might join you. Imagine soaring that close to the earth!" He caught himself, and his voice lost its enthusiasm. "Louise says they're learning on some old army crates and those wouldn't be much fun to fly."

During the recital, Andrews became more and more interested and so did John.

"Have you ever gone up with Louise?" Andrews asked.

"Hell no. She won't even tell me where this flying school is. I only found out about it by accident. I don't know what the big secret is. But if you'd like to go, Gabriel, I'll find out for you and go, too."

"Oh, yes, do! I would love to do that. It sounds so exciting!" Gabriel had not picked up on Andrew's interest or John's disapproval.

"How about some dancing, until you can fly that is?" John all but pulled her away.

Before they left the group, Armad said to John, "By the way," he looked at Andrews, "I think I figured the reason for those number mix-ups was what we expected. The Army Hazardous Substance Management Systems newsletter said they were upgrading the software for the army sites. Those numbers got mixed up 'cause some of the chemical containers were being moved when the software was checking the numbers."

Later that night after John had deposited Gabriel and Rene back home and seen them safely to bed, he stole down to the den and found Chloe waiting for him "What did you find out?" He asked.

"It looks like we're on the right track. The Anderson Brother's Construction Company works both places, Tooele and Newport. They interestingly enough also own a subsidiary, an oil delivery company, ABC Oil, listed separately, that made an oil delivery to the Newport Indiana facility recently. The interesting part is that some of their large oil containers look very much like those one-ton chemical containers that Richard and Don were describing at Aberdeen. Here's another interesting point, Anderson is owned by the Bay of Bengal Trading Company, a foreign company, English or Indian I think. Can you go to Newport tomorrow to check the containers? Richard plans to go to Tooele and see if any of the M55-rockets are missing?"

"Good Lord. You think they've switched the chemical tanks for oil tanks." John sat down hard.

"I'm afraid that's what it appears to be. We'll know soon."

"Look. Can you keep an eye on Gabriel while I'm gone? She wants to take flying lessons and Armad seems to be encouraging her."

"Why in heaven's name?" Chloe sat up straighter.

"It seems Armad's little friend, Louise, is taking flying lessons with some crop dusting group. Armad more or less pulled the information out of Louise. She really didn't want to discuss it at the wedding reception. For some reason Gabriel latched on to it, talked about how exciting it would be to fly so low over the fields. Andrews showed up and seemed inordinately interested that Louise had discussed flying. Then Dowell just happened by to tow her off to dance before she could say more."

"Oh dear, are you thinking what I am? What if the chemicals for warfare were loaded onto crop dusting planes?"

"Let's not jump to conclusions. First, let's see if the chemicals are missing. Do you have any leads yet on where the rockets might be?" John slipped his feet out of his shoes and leaned back.

"None. Best get to sleep. Tomorrow will be a full day. Hope Richard is enjoying this one night. He'll not have a chance to for a long while. God knows what he will tell Harriet to get away on the second day of their wedding." Chloe rose from the sofa.

John picked up his shoes. "That, my dear Chloe, is the advantage of marrying a doctor. They understand being called out!"

CHAPTER NINE

"My but you look wide awake this morning. I find the sight of you sitting here at my breakfast table very pleasant." John bent over Gabriel and gave her a peck on the cheek.

"You had better be careful or you'll give me ideas." Then her eyes sparkling, she added, " I got a call from Armad this morning; he was so pleased with himself. He said he was at work but he had found the location of Louise's airfield and was going home to lord over her how smart he was and see if she wanted to go out there with us. He also said he was surprised. Louise had told him they were learning on old rickety planes, but he found out the planes housed at that airport are state of the art. He thought she didn't want him to worry." Gabriel was very excited and spoke quickly.

John scowled. "Gabriel, I wish you wouldn't do this. This could be quite dangerous. You don't know how capable or safety-conscious these flight instructors are. Have you mentioned it to Rene?"

She tossed her head. "I wish people would stop telling me what to do and not to do!"

"Remember what happened in London. All I know about Armad is that he is on this committee with me. He seems like a decent chap, but something makes we worried about him." John felt constrained about what he could and could not say. The mention of 'London' had sobered Gabriel a good deal. She looked down at her plate. "I'll tell you what. Promise me that if you go, you'll take Chloe with you."

"So now I need a chaperone. Maybe I should ask my father to go, too, or you would like to come along?" She rose from the table.

"Look, sit down. I'm just worried about your safety. You're so trusting. Just do this: find out where Armad is taking you and tell Chloe, okay? The truth is I'm becoming quite fond of you and don't want anything to happen to you." John found this last sentence hard to say. "I'm going to have to be out of town today, but when I come back, I want to talk to you about the future, our future." He astonished himself how nervous he felt; he all but gulped.

Her voice and face softened. This would fit her plans perfectly and was just what she wanted. She reached over and patted his arm. "All right. For you I will ask Chloe to go and if she can't, I'll tell her where we will be. Satisfied?"

Rene's appearance forestalled any further comment. "Bon jour." He smiled at what he thought was a nice tableau. *Yes, I would like to see Gabriel settled so nicely with John, a very satisfying circumstance. I would actually prefer a Frenchman, but his mother is French! A very comfortable circumstance he has here, I could come down to breakfast to my family*. He smiled at the thought. *John could make her happy and protect her even from herself. I might even think - what would it be like to be a grandfather?* His mood was mellow.

"Papa, do try the blueberry pancakes that Mrs. Adams made. They are delicious." Gabriel swallowed the last bite and mumbled with her mouth full.

"You all must excuse me today. I have to be out of town on business, but I'll be back later tonight in time for a late dinner I hope you can join me." John paused and considered how much to say. He looked meaningfully at Gabriel.

"We'll plan to eat late. We are flattered you'd like our company. You can call if you're detained." Rene proposed.

"Done." John glanced back, wondering if he should have said more. His cell phone rang and cut off any further talk.

"Hello, John. This is Mozley."

"Excuse me a moment," he spoke into the phone. Then John turned and explained to Rene and Gabriel with his hand over the receiver, "Business. I'll take this in the library." As soon as the door was closed, he continued speaking. "Sorry, I had company. Now we can talk."

"I just got a call from the State Department. I have to go back. Something about a terrorist threat in Russia. I think the U.S. is cutting back on our financial help to them to get them to destroy their chemical weapons. Someone in the Russian mafia wants to buy some of their CW's. Anyway, it's a big mess and I have to go to Moscow. Anything I can do for you before I go?"

"Yes. Could you arrange for me to get into the Newport, Indiana facility and Richard to get into the Tooele, Utah place?"

"Sure. I'll call my secretary, Jack Nichols. Nice guy. I'll get him to fax your application to get into the army sites. Call him at my office and give him the dates you want to go. I'm a little concerned that this all happened in Russia at the same time we're closing in on these misplaced weapons, too much of a coincidence. We must be getting close. Also, someone pretty high up is involved to have made this 'coincidence' occur. So be careful and warn Richard and Chloe!"

"Will do. Be careful yourself. Could you tell Nichols I plan to go today? Richard can call him with his dates. Guess we won't be in touch if you 're in Moscow. Good luck!" John replaced the phone with a feeling of dread. Mozley had access to some government places they might need and knowledge of whom to call for what. They had counted on his contacts. Things were heating up and they kept losing some key players.

After checking in with Mozley's secretary, John got a ticket to Terra Haute and arranged for a rented car at Terra Haute airport to drive to the Newport Chemical Depot. The flight to Terra Haute was uneventful. He picked up a small Honda, found Indiana State Highway 63, and picked up some local music on radio station WLEZ at 1027 FM. About two miles south of Newport, John saw the large

Newport Chemical Depot (NECD) surrounded by a single chain-link barbed-wire fence. A huge stone pedestal with a black sign and white letters announced Newport Chemical Depot. *You can't accuse them of trying to hide the place*, he thought. The entrances were guarded and he could see intrusion detection devices and television monitors in every nook and cranny. The large lot to the side surrounded by double fences he assumed was the storage area. John remembered Richard had told him the army guards at the CW and CT locations were the only ones with permanent orders of shoot to kill.

A very helpful army private escorted him into the registration building for him to pick up his faxed entrance permit, and then took him to the Commander's office. A short, balding man rose. "How do you do. Matthews here." He extended his hand.

"Thank you for seeing me. I'm Professor Davis on the HSD committee to check on some number mix-up of the CT's. Do you have several minutes to answer a few questions that I have and could you tell me something about this facility?"

"Yes, of course. I have been notified of your committee. We've been wondering when you'd come. Tempest in a teapot as far as I can see, but of course procedure must be observed. Would you care to do an inspection?"

"No thank you. I don't think that is necessary at this time. I understand you have a good deal of VX here." He sat in a chair that Matthews indicated and waited for his host to begin.

Matthews settled down into his chair, lighted a cigarette and offered John one. When he shook his head, Matthews leaned back and started a recital he had probably given many times. "The Newport Chemical Depot, the NECD or Depot as it's called, in 1995 was reporting to the U.S. Army Chemical and Biological Defense command that now is a part of the U.S. Army Material command. While we're contract operated we're government owned. The contracting operator is Mason & Hanger in Lexington, Kentucky. They've got 222 full time employees. We've got about 7 acres plus another 1400 acres in easement.

"In 1941 Du Pont was awarded the contract to construct an RDX facility. RDX by the way is an explosive. They completed it in 1943. The cost was $45 million plus. Du Pont went to manufacturing heavy water and in 1951 Liberty Powder Defense Corporation of East Alton, Illinois took over two of the five RDX lines and of course their facilities for about four and a half million. They were contracted to the Army and worked there until 1957. From '57 to '60 the site was not used.

"In 1959 the Army gave a contract to FMC Corporation in New York to build a facility to produce VX. They completed the plant in 1961 at a cost of sixteen and a half million in the area where they formerly produced heavy water. Of course when they started producing the nerve agent VX, they had to bring in some disposal specialists to the site. FMC produced VX under Army contract until 1968 when VX was placed on standby.

"The army produced its entire stockpile of VX at Newport. All kinds of munitions, land mines, spray tanks and rockets, were shipped in by rail, filled with VX and shipped out worldwide to U.S. defense sites. Nixon halted production of VX in 1968 and halted shipments in 1969. The final two batches of 1,269 tons are in storage here. We decontaminated the production plant all we could, fenced it off, and left it to rust.

"The VX stockpiled at NECD is in steel one-ton containers called TC's, 1,690 of 'em. They're six and a half feet long and three feet in diameter, the sides are solid steel and a half inch thick, the ends are an inch thick. Why, just empty they weigh in at 1,600 pounds and can hold 170 gallons. The TC's here have a layer of nitrogen gas that takes up 10% of the space. Those babies can take outside pressure of twenty five times our atmosphere and inside they can take 500 pounds per square inch. We stack them in rows three containers high and clamp 'em together to keep 'em stable. They're put on concave wooden cradles. They're all together in a warehouse made out of corrugated steel sheet metal supported by steel beams. I tell you, our men are really trained in handling this stuff."

He shifted in his chair and lit another cigarette. "Not only the area has 24 hour per day monitoring for detecting chemical release, the storage building has four Automatic Continuous Air Monitoring Systems called ACAMS. If any leakage at all was spotted all sorts of alarms go off, you can hear the alarms and see all kinds of lights and alerts.

"We'll store VX here until they get that pilot neutralization plant up and running. You still with me, Son?" John nodded. "Well, the Parsons-Allied Signal team's going to use a low-temperature low-pressure chemical neutralization process and then a high temperature water oxidation. That reduces the neutralized product to water and salt and some organic salts. Once the agent is removed, the containers will be cleaned and decontaminated and shipped to other places for recycling. Probably to standard metal recyclers. You got any questions?"

"Well, yes I do. You had some work done here by the Anderson Construction Company. Also, you had some oil deliveries by one of their subsidiaries, ABC Oil. Could you give me those dates? Were they admitted anywhere near the storage facility?"

"I'll be happy to look up the dates. They had no business being near the storage facility, I don't think, but I can check. As for the oil, we run a lot of machinery so we do use lots of oil. How about we have some lunch while I get some people to dig up that information? We could go into Clinton to the Dreamland Café or to Janet's Family Restaurant in Montezuma or if you want we can eat here at the base. The food's not as good but it's closer."

"Why don't we eat here? I have some friends staying with me in D.C. and I'd like to get back as soon as I can." The cigarette smoke was beginning to get to him. Fervently he wished for a walk in fresh air.

"No problem. I'll get someone on this and we can head on up to the mess." Matthews coughed and rose from his chair. "It's not far and the weather is okay. We can talk as we go." He stepped into the outer office and conferred with his secretary.

"How did they produce VX?' John asked as they left the building.

"Watch your step there. We're putting in new sidewalks. VX was produced in four steps, zero though three. The facilities for the first three steps are already removed; I mean they've been taken care of. Step three took place inside the storage area that will be abolished by 2007, God willing. Step three is where the stuff was combined to make the actual VX. We still have a few of the employees who were here when they produced VX." He held the door for John. "We go though the cafeteria line. Pick up a tray."

"Wow, this looks good!" John eyed the fried chicken and piles of fresh vegetables and potatoes piled up in huge heaps behind a glass counter.

"Yeah, mid-west, best fresh foods in the nation! I grew up on the stuff. You can keep your New York fancy food or that foreign stuff. I was stationed in Japan and I never could get used to all that rice. Thank God we didn't have to use chopsticks in the mess. I'd have starved to death. Food kept falling off before I could get it to my mouth," Matthews piled his plate high. "Come on, we can sit over here." He led the way to a pine picnic-type table.

"Did any other members of the committee I'm on ever come here?" John put his tray down and straddled a bench. The rest of the tables were crowded, but Matthews had chosen an empty one over by the window.

"Seems to me a Mr. Andrews did come, but it was before my time. I've only been here about four years." Matthews lit another cigarette and smoked between bites.

"Who's doing the neutralization? Wait," John held up his hand. "I'm going to go back and get another piece of that chicken." Matthews grinned as John walked back to the cafeteria line.

When he returned, Matthews took up John's question as if he'd never left. "Parsons Infrastructure and Technology Group, Inc., they have a team partnership with Allied Signal to do the whole shebang: design, build, operate and close. They got a $295 million dollar contract. You didn't get the chocolate cake. It's the best. Now my mother was a good cook but even she couldn't equal this! Here, wait right where you are. I'm going back for a piece." He rose with difficulty and returned in several minutes laden with four pieces of cake. "You're a growing boy. You need some calories." He laughed, gave John two pieces and kept two for himself.

John inhaled the cake. "I always heard army food wasn't good. You can't beat this."

"Some New Englander probably started that 'cause they couldn't get a special kind of fish. Those New Englanders, they are the hardest-to-please bunch!"

"Can we walk around outside when we finish?" John asked.

"Sure. See over there?" The Commander pointed out a window. "Those are bulk storage tanks where they kept the VX before they put them into the TC's or munitions. We've eight empty ones of those. Just sitting there."

Once outside, Matthews pointed up to what looked like two chimneys joined together in three places by pipes. "Those are scrubber towers. When they produced VX here, they used scrubber towers to clean air from inside a building before the air was released.

"Does your wife worry about you working here? I should have asked are you married?" John viewed the tanks with awe.

"Yeah. Been married twenty-seven years. Naw. She says my smoking will kill me before this stuff gets to me." He leaned back and laughed and then had a coughing fit.

"Did I tell you, the Coast Guard has a 101 acre permit for its LORAN-C Station? That stands for Long Range Aerial Navigation." He spluttered between coughs.

About an hour later, seated in his office, a secretary brought in a sheaf of papers. "Okay, here's the dope. "Well, I'll be. You must be a mind reader. Anderson Construction was here just two weeks ago to reinforce one of those steel beams in that warehouse I was telling you about. They had some very big, heavy machinery in there. Had to, those beams are real giants. But we had people watching them all the time. And yes, they did deliver some oil to get those machines to work." He squinted at the page.

"Sir, do you know which beams they worked on?" John leaned forward.

"Let's see. Yeah, it was the ones way in the back. Took a lot of finagling I bet to get to them." Matthews lit another cigarette.

"Sir, could you check those TC's close to where they worked?" John leaned further from his chair.

"You mean to see if there's a leak?" Matthews dowsed his cigarette in an ashtray already overflowing.

"No, Sir. I mean to check to see if those TC's contain VX rather then oil." John leaned back.

Slowly the full meaning of what he was implying hit home. “Now just a minute, Son. You’re insinuating that we’re not careful here. Why we have twenty-four hour watch all around.”

“And I’m sure you are careful, but as a protection to you and your site, perhaps you could verify that the TC’s have not been tampered with. When you have a lot of big machinery and drop cloths and all, things can get mixed up. For example, those oil tanks could be made to look just like the VX tanks. All you have to do is put some marked plastic overlays to those tanks and the switch would be invisible. They’re what about six and a half feet by three feet? Not too hard to manipulate. If all the TC’s have VX, you have nothing to worry about, but if someone made a switch with one of those tanks, then it’s better for you to find out now rather then be blamed for it after some monkey business goes on.” John sat beside the desk, his elbows leaning on the top.

“I see what you’re saying. Better safe then sorry. I’ll get some boys working on it right away, but it’ll be awhile before we can test all those in the vicinity. Give me your phone number and I’ll call you as soon as it’s finished.”

John handed him his card. “Thanks for all your help and that great lunch. I really truly hope for all our sakes the tanks have VX.”

“Chloe, thank God I found you alone.” The clock on the library wall showed seven, Chloe was seated at the desk going over some papers. Already darkness was invading the windows. “I just got back from Newport. Things don’t look too good. I’ll talk fast in case either Rene or Gabriel comes in. The construction company with lots of heavy machinery and an ABC oil truck worked on the building where the one-ton containers of VX are stored. The Army’s going to check the contents of the containers in the vicinity of where the construction people worked and let me know as soon as they can. What have you heard here?”

“Richard called. Rester continues to come in and out of consciousness. But from what they can get from his mutterings, the M55 rockets either were taken from Tooele or are there under wraps. He planned to fly out this afternoon.”

They heard the front door open and close. Rene came into the room. "Ah, you did get back in time for dinner. I was rather late myself, had some paper work to get over to the embassy. Where is Gabriel?"

Chloe looked startled. "I though she was with you. I had some shopping to do and when I went to her room, she was gone."

John and Chloe exchanged worried looks. John rushed into the hall calling, "Mrs. Adams."

"Yes, Sir. Oh, am glad you got back. Did you have a good trip?"

"Fine, thank you. Do you know where Miss Beaumond is?"

"Oh, she went out around four. She said, now let me see if I got it right, a friend of yours, Armad I think she said, was supposed to pick her and another young lady up but he hadn't come by, so she was going out on her own. Something about flying lessons. She said she'd promised you she'd leave the address for her grandmother. She was going to put it on the table in the hall, but I put it in my pocket so as not to lose it. Here it is."

CHAPTER TEN

"My Dear, thank you for going to the airport with me to see my sisters off. I know it was early. They really liked you and I am so glad. That means a great deal to me." Harriet reached over and nestled her head against his shoulder. "You know this house is very comfortable and strangely enough, snug, even though it is so big." The early afternoon sun traced patters on the Kashan rug at their feet. "Wasn't it sweet of Sarah to leave dinner in the frig for us? She said she thought we should have the place to ourselves for a while, such a thoughtful person."

"I'm not so sure about your sister Hannah. I think she views me with great suspicion." He stroked her hair savoring the little time he knew they would have together this week.

"Well, Hannah wanted me to marry her brother-in-law and go back to live near them. She didn't approve of my work in the CDC. But really basically, I think it's the big sister syndrome. She wants to look after me." She laughed.

"So do I," he whispered. As she nestled closer, the cell phone in his pocket rang just under where her head rested. "Oh, no!"

Richard reached into his pocket as she pulled away. The voice was loud and clear. "Hello, Richard this is Mozley. Been trying to get you. Two things. I'm leaving momentarily for Russia. State has called me back. The U.S. is pulling some money out of the help they promised Russia to dismantle its CW's and the Russian mafia is stepping in. Messy. So Captain Mozley to the rescue. Just talked with Johnny this morning. He's off to Newport. The second thing, Rester is coming and going into consciousness, but we got the fact that the M55 rockets either are at or were taken from Tooele. Oh yeah, one other thing, he mentioned Dowell's name! Nothing else, just his name. I tried to get Dowell but his office said he'd left for Tooele. I called my secretary, Jack Nichols, and he'll fax your papers to get into the Deseret Chemical Depot at Tooele. Let him know when you're leaving. Got to run, plane taking off. Love to the missus, you lucky dawg!"

Slowly Richard closed the phone. From the look on his face, Harriet sighed. She knew what was coming.

"Look, you're going to hate me, but I've got to go out to Utah. I promise I'll come back as soon as I can. Hold my place on the sofa and don't tell Hannah I deserted you on day two or she'll come and haul you off!" He tried to make light but his face was sad.

"Why don't I come with you? I have the rest of the week off from Smithwick. I promise not to get in the way," she suggested.

For a moment Richard hesitated. More then anything he wanted her company, but he remembered Dowell. If their paths crossed and Dowell was cornered, God knew what would happen. "No, you'd better stay here. This won't take long. Honest, I'll try and get back tomorrow."

"From Utah? You've got to be kidding!" She laughed a mirthless sound.

"Listen, I would get back in two days, three at the most even if I were sent to the moon!" And he hugged her tightly.

Richard sat staring out the windows at the majestic mountains and broad expansive valleys. He couldn't believe in such a short time he had been in Virginia and now just twelve miles south of Tooele, Utah. Jack Nichols had understood the rush and gotten him on an air force jet as well as doing all the paperwork to get him into the Tooele Chemical Agent Disposal Facility at the Deseret Chemical Depot in Stockton. Right now he was trying to keep his attention on the tall, thin man speaking.

"As soon as we realized the rockets were missing we called the U.S. Army Program Manager for Chemical Demilitarization, that's the PMCD, and they referred us to Mr. Mozley, said he was handling the mix-up. I tried to explain this was not a number mix-up but missing rockets, but I couldn't get through the bureaucracy there. Thank God you got here. Maybe you can explain to them what's going on. My name is Parkinson by the way, site program manager!" The tall man had stopped pacing back and forth and extended his hand.

This was the first time Richard had seen an army old timer so distraught. He judged Parkinson to be about forty, maybe older, nervous, blue eyes, thinning hairline, but straight carriage. "Tell me how this happened." Richard tried to keep his tone even.

"We've been working in close cooperation with independent agencies, state regulators and program partners to dispose of the chemical weapons stored at Deseret Chemical Depot. We at the Tooele Chemical Agent Disposal Facility, that's TOCDF, want to eliminate the chemical weapons stored here since 1942 and protect our workers, the community and environment."

"Fine," Richard interrupted. "Just tell me what happened!" *Why do they always talk like alphabet soup and take so long to get to the point,* he thought.

"While the plant was gearing up for VX processing, a worker was exposed to Sarin GB in July. Immediately, the Army stopped all operation at TOCDF voluntarily. We investigated all procedures and corrected those that needed it. We've added more training for site operators and managers and beefed up our safety program. All the critical changes have been verified by safety and operating reviews. We restarted on the day shift only, phasing in the other shifts so we'd restart with everybody on board, all prepared in processing and non-routine activities. That exposure in July really shook everybody up and we saw that we needed some changes." Parkinson stopped pacing and sipped from a cup of coffee. “Oh, say, I’m sorry, would you like some coffee?”

“Yes, thank you. I’m still on Eastern Time.” For some reason Richard felt washed out after all the past week activities.

Parkinson went to a thermos on a corner table, poured some coffee into one of a stack of mugs and inquired, “Black?” When Richard nodded he walked over, gave him the cup, and started pacing again.

“And then…” Richard prompted.

“Oh, yes.” Parkinson continued, “When we were doing the revisions of procedures we started an Employee Concern Program to identify and find solutions to any concerns the workers have. This is a team effort and we have weeks of training in safe handling and delivery of munitions from their storage locations to the disposal facility. We started destruction of the chemical weapons with Sarin nerve agent weapons since Sarin was the most dangerous to the public, more dangerous then VX or mustard we thought. We got rid of 6,000 tons of Sarin. We moved on to the VX agent, beginning with the M55 rockets. We have the largest stockpile of VX by weight in the U.S.; over 1,300 tons contained in seven different munitions types, that’s 30% of the original U.S. stockpile. When we finish with VX we start on the mustard destruction. So far we’ve destroyed 8,082 tons of chemical agents. That’s 25% of the U.S. stockpile.

“Well, in our Employee Concerns Group one of our people pointed out a discrepancy between the number of M55’s destroyed, the number of ones remaining and the total number to begin with. We started adding up the numbers and by Jove, four are missing! And to think it was a civilian who noticed it! I feel so ashamed!” He emphasized the last sentence by setting his cup down so hard that the contents spilled out and he had to sop it off his desk with some paper towels. “We’ve been over and over the lists, checking numbers. We’ve searched all the depositories and we can’t find where those four are!”

“Several questions.” Richard sipped his coffee. “First, was Major Dowell here during any of this procedure?”

Parkinson looked startled. "Let me check. Jean?" He called into the speakerphone on his desk, "bring in the register of visitors for the last year."

A pert, rather chubby redhead in her late thirties or early forties came in with a large book and placed it on the desk. Parkinson nodded and she left the room. He ran his finger down the page, "Yes, he did, about two months ago."

"Is Dowell here now?" Richard was becoming anxious.

Parkinson consulted the register again. "Nope. Not signed in since that last time, two months ago."

"This is strange, because his office said he was headed here and gave this as his destination. Do you know where he stays when he comes out?" Richard questioned.

Parkinson scratched his head. Again he consulted his desk speakerphone. "Jean, could you come in?" When Jean was just inside the door, he started questioning. "Do you know where Dowell stays when he comes here?" When she turned red faced and started to bristle, he apologized, "I said that badly. I mean, did he leave a motel number where we could get in touch with him for meetings when he's here?"

"All our visitors stay at the Hampton Inn in Tooele," she replied tight-lipped.

"What about the Anderson Construction people. Were they here the same time as Dowell?" Richard was standing over the register and thumbing over the pages. "Yep, here's a Mr. Risotto. He's listed as the Anderson rep." He turned to Jean, "Could you see if either Mr. Risotto or Major Dowell are registered now at that Hampton Inn? Could you ask in such a way that we ascertain that he is there without contacting him directly?" She looked at him with wide eyes. "May she use this phone, Parkinson?"

By now, both he and Jean were transfixed. "Yes, of course." He handed Jean the phone.

She reached for the phone book on the shelf behind his desk and nervously looked up the number, cognizant that they were both watching her, and dialed the number, her hands shaking but her voice firm when, in her best professional voice she asked, "I'm setting up some meetings, could you tell me if either Major Dowell or Mr.

Risotto have signed in yet?" She waited. "No, no message. I'll call back tomorrow and speak with them. I'm leaving work now for the day." She hung up the phone and turned to Richard. "They have both signed in but are not in their rooms. I think most people who come here eat at the dining room in the hotel. It's about dinner time."

"Thank you. That was well done." Richard smiled at her.

She looked at Parkinson, "Will there be anything else, Sir?"

"No, thank you, Jean." Parkinson waited until she left. "You obviously believe Dowell has something to do with this?"

"Yes, I do. We have reason to believe that Dowell is connected in some way. You've met the man. What do you think of him?" Richard sat down again.

"Interesting contradiction. He's very rigid when he's here, very army and all that, but I saw him at the bar with some of the construction men and he was hail-fellow, well met. Funny, he was out of uniform then. I didn't think much about it at the time. You know every fellow needs to let his hair down sometimes. It just struck me how different he seemed, like two separate personalities. Not someone I'd want for a friend. He seems to rub people the wrong way. Jean for instance, whenever he comes she appears angry all the time. I think Dowell fancies himself as a lady's man." Parkinson stroked his chin.

"What kind of security force do you have here?" Richard asked.

"All these disposal sites have first rate Army surveillance teams."

"Good. This is my plan. We'll need about eight men, strong and good shots…"

Parkinson interrupted him, "I'm afraid we can't do that. You see army personnel and the CIA, too, for that matter, aren't allowed to participate in off base activities that place them in danger unless called out by the president or some such. But, I could get us some state tactical squad agents I know who are good men, trustworthy and capable."

"What about yourself? Won't you be in trouble? You're army."

"I'll be out of uniform and just hope I don't get caught. I feel responsible for this whole mess. I'll simply be acting in my capacity as a citizen not an officer." Parkinson drew himself up.

"Okay," Richard continued, "I hope to follow Dowell and this Risotto and hope they will lead us to the rockets. I'm assuming the rockets are still here or why else would Dowell have come? And why not sign in? I'll need these men in plain clothes and armed. I believe Dowell has the rockets stashed someplace nearby. Probably removed them during the scare you had from the Sarin contamination in July. My guess is they will try and move them out at night. If you have reported the rockets missing, then your message possibly got to the ears of whoever is organizing these thefts so they may try to move them tonight."

"Thefts? Are there more then one?" Parkinson paled.

"So far, we have aborted two instances of chemical weapons taken from other sites. Could you have these security men ready right away? I would like to have that motel staked out by dark." Richard picked up his briefcase.

"Yes. And I will come, too. I don't ask any men to take chances I'm not willing to share. I suggest that I set this in motion and then perhaps you'll join me for dinner?"

"Thank you, yes I'd like that. Could we eat somewhere inconspicuous? And could we ask your secretary to join us? She has overheard what we've been saying. I don't want anyone to alert Dowell. She might inadvertently mention this conversation to someone, who would then mention it to a friend of Dowell's."

"I'll ask her to order in Chinese. Actually, I've been wanting to ask her out for dinner and haven't gotten up my nerve." He looked embarrassed, his tone was confidential and a red blush began to creep up his neck. "I'm not married you see, never have been. I've had to move around a lot and the boss-secretary thing and all can get messy. But this would be a good way, don't you think?" As he left the room, Richard shook his head. Amid the seriousness of the situation, to find a shy army man, one willing to face danger with his men, but too shy to ask his secretary out was ludicrous. Harriet would appreciate the humor in it all. He opened his brief case to ascertain that his service revolver was still there.

"Just spread everything out on the desk and we can help ourselves, Jean. I really appreciate your staying late." Parkinson moved all his papers off the top of his desk, piled them messily on a chair, and helped spread the food.

Richard held out his hand. "Hi, I'm Richard Moore and I take it you are Jean. Jean what?"

The busy secretary hesitated and then shook hands smiling, "Jean Martin. I've been here about two years." She looked at Parkinson, " I didn't know what to order so I just ordered my favorites, General Tso's chicken, Moo Shu Pork and Shrimp with Cashew Nuts and of course rice."

"Incredible. Those are my favorites, too!" Parkinson looked up surprised. Richard refrained from mentioning those were most peoples' favorites. "I must say though, there's a Thai restaurant in Tooele that I just love," he added.

"On North Main, right down the street from the Mexican place!" Jean stared. "But I've never seen you there. I hesitate to go by myself. So often, I wait until one of my girl friends is going."

"Well, Parkinson, I think you owe Miss Martin a dinner after making her work late tonight," interposed Richard. *Cupid's little helper*, he thought.

"What a good idea. How about next week, Jean?" Parkinson was reddening all the way up to his receding hairline.

"I'd like that," she said. "I'm free on Friday."

"Friday it is. We'd better eat fast. Richard wants to be out by dark." He dove into the pork to hide his embarassment.

When they had finished and Jean was clearing the left-overs into the other room, Parkinson muttered lowly so she wouldn't hear, "You said dark, but just to be safe I had two of our men sign into the motel. They're reading newspapers in the lobby and two more are parked outside in back. Their orders are to call us if Dowell or Risotta leave. It'll take us about thirty minutes to get to Tooele and park. Four other men will meet us there." Parkinson removed his uniform jacket, slipped on a black windbreaker and baseball cap.

"Good work. Are you armed?" Richard added. Parkinson patted his coat pocket.

"Brrr, it gets cold in Utah when they turn off the sun." Richard muttered as he rubbed his arms. Even inside the car, the temperature had dropped. *Damn I wish I'd brought a heavier coat*, he thought.

As if he read his thoughts, Parkinson volunteered, "There's a jacket on the back seat. Help yourself. It's old but warm. I keep it there when I go hunting. By the way, thanks for the nudge back there. I mean about asking Jean to dinner. I've never been handy around women."

"Who is? I just got married yesterday and I'm no spring chicken." Richard didn't add that he'd had lots of opportunities.

"You're kidding! You mean this is your wedding trip or should have been?" Parkinson exclaimed.

"My wife (*damn, I like the sound of that,* he thought) is a doctor and very understanding. Just hope her sisters don't hear about it. Oops, looks like our men are heading out. We can't follow too close or leave too soon. Looks like they're heading for the Desert Depot. Where are your men?"

"See that green sedan coming in from the other direction? That's some of them. They'll park and the guys in the blue station wagon will pull out. Nobody suspects a station wagon. Everybody thinks of it as a family car." With that statement, Parkinson rose in Richard's esteem, defining himself as a man who thinks and understands other's thinking. "We have a car parked at the intersection of highway 73 and 36. The station wagon turns there onto the road Dowell doesn't take and the other car will pick up the trail and follow Dowell. I think we'd better get going, too."

The moon was just beginning to show up outlining the mountain range and the distant valleys. The black car ahead was picking up speed. Of a sudden it made a swift u-turn and barely missed them as it headed back in the other direction. "Damn, but that was clever." Parkinson muttered in grudging admiration and picking up his phone, he punched in the number. "Pete, they're headed back toward you at the motel. Keep an eye out. I'll phone Sam up at the intersection and have him come down this way." Which he proceeded to do. "If they get on I-80 we'll have more trouble keeping them insight."

A few more miles up the highway the black car pulled off to the right near a parking lot by the railway tracks and parked. Parkinson slowed down as they passed by. In the lot was a large semi trailer with the words "Anderson Construction" on it. The truck was just parked as if the driver had pulled over to take a snooze. As Richard looked back he saw two men get out of the black sedan and get into the cab of the truck. "They're going to head for I-80." Parkinson picked up the phone. "Okay, everybody, head this way, we've got to try to get to this truck when it hits the interstate to keep track of them. If we lose them, I've got their license number, but we're not going to lose them! Understand?

" I don't see how we can make it. Parkinson, there is no way for a car or even several cars to stop a truck that size!' Richard was shouting over the motor.

Parkinson smiled over to him and reaching under the seat he brought out a small C B radio. Nimbly, with one hand, he hooked it up and started transmitting, "Any trucker buddies out there on I-80? I've got myself a little problem here and need your help. Some Eastern dude who's out to bust up our union has hijacked one of my trucks. It has a big sign painted on the side 'Anderson Construction' and it's turning onto I-80 from 36 and headed East toward Salt lake City. Anybody see it? I'd sure appreciate any help you could give me to get my truck back. This is Lonely Al. Over." Richard tried not to laugh, *Lonely Al is certainly a good handle for Parkinson*, he thought.

Within a few minutes a voice came back over a crackling noise. "Hi Lonely, Black Jack here. I see the critter, he's right in front of me. I'll just give him a nudge if you say the word. Over."

"I see him too, Lonely. I'm right along side. What do you want? Tar Eyes. Over."

"Boys, I sure appreciate your help. Maybe you could encourage him to pull over to the siding and stop. I'm in a blue sedan behind you guys. Don't get out of your cabs, boys. These dudes are armed. Lonely. Over."

A large semi trailer moving van gently nudged the Anderson truck to the side. At 60 miles per hour he kept up a steady intrusion into the lane of the Anderson truck, which finally pulled onto the shoulder. The van then pulled out in front and parked with the motor running. A food chain freezer truck pulled in very close behind the

Anderson truck, blocking any chance of Dowell backing up and escaping. Parkinson pulled in behind him.

Parkinson got out on his side of the car and John from the other side just as two other cars pulled up behind him. Four men got out. Parkinson and the four men edged along the side of the truck just as Dowell jumped down and went running forward toward the semi trailer moving van, red-faced and swearing, "Stupid fool, what did you force me off for? What's going on here? Some jackass game of tag? Get out you moron. Who the hell do you think you are? I'll have your fuc……" He stopped mid-sentence as Parkinson sprang and grabbed him just as he reached the cab of the truck. Two other men appeared and pinned his arms behind his back. Risotto in the cab saw what was happening and tried to get out the other side and make a run for it, as Richard stepped up and pushed the barrel of his gun into his head. "Don't do anything I'll regret," he growled.

Parkinson signaled his men to take both men back to his car. He followed them back to his car. From under the front seat he retrieved two boxes of cigars and then pulled out of the trunk two gallon-jugs of whiskey. He went to first one truck cab and then another. To each he said, "Boy, I do really appreciate your help. Indeed I do. Please take this with my thanks. I think you just saved my union. Much obliged. No need to get down. We've got everything under control now. Much obliged." He returned their waves as they pulled back onto the highway.

Richard was impressed. "Well done. Like me you thought they would go south. But you had that all planned just in case they went either way. Neatest bit of work I've seen in a long time. And the whiskey and cigars, nice attention to detail." Then he smiled, "Jean Martin doesn't have a chance when you have strategy like that!"

They were standing at the rear of the truck. Parkinson said, "Let's see what we have here." He and Richard opened the back doors of the truck and heaved themselves up. Under layers of camouflage blankets were the missing M55 Rockets and their launchers.

"Thank God," Richard gasped. "Let's see what our friends have to say to this."

As they approached the cars, they could hear Risotta shouting, "He made me do this. Said these things were polluting the water and we needed to give the White House a dose of its own medicine. We weren't going to fire them. Just show them what could happen. How they could be swiped right from under their nose!"

Dowell snarled, "Shut up you fool." He turned to Richard. "I refuse to say anything."

Richard suggested, "Let's take them back to TOCDF and turn them over to the army. Can anyone drive this truck back?"

Parkinson said, "I can. I drove a truck in Vietnam."

"Why am I not surprised?" Richard chuckled. He got in the driver's seat of the blue sedan, Risotta was placed in one car and Dowell in another and all started the caravan back to headquarters.

They were surprised to see Jean Martin waiting for them when they finally staggered into Parkinson's office. "I forgot to tell you that I had gotten some ice cream for dessert." She looked at Parkinson and the nervous worry was plain on her face.

"You mean you waited here all this time just to give us dessert?" he was dumbfounded.

I can't believe this guy, Richard thought. *After a brilliant move to get these thugs and he really doesn't know she cares. Holy cow!* "Parkinson, the least you can do is drive her home. My God, it's late and she's waited all this time for us. That is after you eat the ice cream of course. Me, I'm going to try and hitch a ride back to D.C. with one of the army planes. I'll have company of course. Two guys we met tonight will be going back, too." He gave Parkinson a knowing look and added, "I have a honeymoon to catch up on."

Richard held his cell phone close to his ear to try and drown out the sound of the plane reviving up to take off. "Honey, I'm on my way home (*the word sounded so sweet to him*). We got the things we came for. I said I'd be back within three days!"

"Oh Richard, I'm so glad you called. I've been worried. I just got off the phone to John. He said to tell you the container held oil. You'd know what he meant. Also, Armad was to pick up Gabriel and Louise and he's gone missing. I think Gabriel's gone to some airfield to find them."

CHAPTER ELEVEN

Armad had promised to pick her up and then never showed. Gabriel was not used to being stood up, especially not by a really unattractive man, a nerd and with a beard yet! She tried to decide what she should do. *I can't just sit here and let John see that I've been passed over. I'm certainly not going to go to Louise and have her think her nerd didn't show. Well, why not go to the airfield myself? I have the address and the money to pay for a lesson. I'll just show them all I don't need supervision as if I were a child. But I promised John I'd leave the address of the airfield. So I'd better do it. At least he seems to like me. Mon Dieu, I want to get back by tonight. I think he's going to propose*. That thought brought a smile to her face.

"Mrs. Adams" she called.

"Yes, Dear." Mrs. Adams dried her hands on a towel as she came into the hall.

"I'm going to an airfield for flying lessons!" She basked in the expression of excitement her words induced in the little housekeeper, who was very impressed. "I promised John I'd leave the address, just in case he or Mrs. Manning want to get in touch." She smiled. "Please tell them I left it on the hall table."

"Oh, no, Miss. It could get knocked off or mail !aid atop it. Here, you just give it to me and I'll see that they get it." Mrs. Adams took the note and stuffed it in her apron pocket.

"Thank you. John said he'd be home later and we're going to wait and have dinner with him when he gets back so I'll be back in plenty of time."

When Gabriel looked for her purse, she couldn't find it. *Damn, it contains my international driver's license.* She spent twenty minutes looking through all the clothes she'd packed before she found it. Then she had to go back to Mrs. Adams to get the car keys to the Volvo that John had left in the driveway for her to use. "Feel free to go anywhere you like. This is one very safe little car," he'd said. She felt such a fool, traipsing back into the house again.

Gabriel left John's home in Georgetown around four and in a very bad temper. She decided to follow the directions Armad had given her over the phone. Since he started from Massachusetts Avenue, she guessed he lived nearby. She found Massachusetts on her map of Washington. The commuter traffic was just building up and she hit the construction work on 7th street just as the rest of the going-home-Washingtonians did. She had studied the map closely while she was waiting for Armad and had estimated the time about an hour. Obviously the trip was going to take longer. At the first construction sign she went a half-mile, exited and got back on Massachusetts and proceeded to take three exits and entrances before she got to Du Pont Circle. At 17th Street she had another detour on to U.S. 50. By this time she realized she'd had no lunch. She didn't see a place to eat on US 1 or I-395. But after the 'Entering Virginia' sign she had hopes. Still no food on I-95! *Mon Dieu*, she thought, *where do Americans stop to eat when they drive? They are all so heavy! No wonder, they have to have enough stored fat on their bodies to sustain them until they can get to a café!*

At exit 133, when she turned onto US 17, which is Warrenton Road, she spotted a small roadside truck stop. The surroundings did not look appetizing, but she was famished. Gabriel took a vacant table by the window so she could keep an eye on the car. Two young men at the counter turned and appraised her figure then smiled at each other approvingly.

"What'll it be, Miss?" The waitress had probably seen her twentieth birthday twenty years ago, but she still tried to keep the impression that it was yesterday.

"Do you have the soup?" Gabriel scanned the menu.

"No, we just have that at lunch or dinner. Since we're between meals hours, I could make you a hotdog or a hamburger." She tapped her foot with the hope that would get Gabriel to make up her mind.

"Do you have a grilled cheese sandwich?" *I cannot believe I'm wasting precious time arguing with this idiot, but I'm so hungry.*

"Yep. What to drink?" The foot tapped again.

"Coffee, please. Black." She viewed the stained tabletop. *That food should be safe. Everything will be cooked so I have less chance of getting food poisoning.* Gabriel tried to smile at the waitress, who was already heading for a phone behind the counter. The loud ring of the phone was the only sound that could compete with the roar of the traffic outside. Gabriel waited while the waitress had a ten-minute conversation at the top of her voice with someone called 'Sam', then for another fifteen agonizing minutes while she poured coffee and grilled two slices of bread. *How could anyone be so slow!*

When the food was set before her, and a bill laid face down beside the plate, she found she could eat only because she was so hungry. Both the sandwich and coffee were luke warm, the bread limp, but she wolfed them down, and then hurried to the cash register.

As she exited, Gabriel heard the waitress comment, "Miss High and Mighty didn't bother to leave a tip. Guess she spends all her money on her clothes."

About fifteen minutes from the grill she spotted a sign almost hidden by overgrown bushes on the right side of the road, 'airport'. *This must be it, but it's so small.* She turned into a dirt road and parked near a hanger. No one seemed to be around. As soon as she stopped the car, another car pulled up behind her and the two men she had seen in the grill got out. Glancing her way, they looked surprised, but they smiled and nodded and walked into the larger of the two buildings. *They must be either the instructors or part of the flying class that Louise is taking.* Gabriel thought.

She opened the door and walked to the counter along the side of the room. The young man behind the counter had been studying a map. He looked up.

"Could you tell me, is this where Louise Wiggins takes flying lessons?' She asked.

"I'm sorry, flying lessons? I don't know about that." He signaled to the other man who walked over.

"Louise's friend Armad Beel gave me directions to this airfield. He said Louise was taking flying lessons." She tried not to sound dumb.

Both men started to laugh. "Louise can fly better then we do. She's not taking lessons, she's been teaching us! Someone's been pulling your leg! Are you here to learn to fly, too?"

"Yes, I heard she was taking lessons to learn to crop dust." Gabriel was beginning to feel uneasy.

At the word 'crop dusting' both men became serious. "But you won't have time to learn to fly. Not if we go up tomorrow."

"But I don't have to go up tomorrow. I could arrange lessons anytime."

The sound of a car driving in and skidding to a stop, kept them from answering. Gabriel looked out and saw Louise getting out of the car and the man with her she recognized as Arnold Andrews. *Thank heaven* she thought, *we can get this cleared up and I can still get back in time for John to propose!*

Both Louise and Andrews stopped in their tracks at the door when they saw her. "What are you doing here?" Louise demanded.

"Armad called today, said he'd found your flying field and offered to take me out here. We thought we'd join your lessons." From the looks exchanged by the four in the room, Gabriel began to feel in the middle of something she didn't understand, but she continued, "Have you seen Armad? He never came by so I just followed his directions. It looks like I've made a mistake. I guess this is a private lesson thing."

Andrews blocked the door and spoke for the first time, "Did you tell anyone you were coming here?"

Defiantly, Gabriel admitted. "Yes, I left a message for John Davis that I was coming to take flying lessons." She turned to

Louise, "It seems I was mistaken; you are not taking the lessons. These gentlemen say you are teaching them to fly! Now if you'll move, I'll leave you."

Andrews turned and locked the door. Then he came back to Gabriel and shoved her into a chair. "That means they'll come looking for her. The chemical container won't be delivered until tonight. The people in the lab in the hanger still have to get it into a dispensable mixture, then load the containers and that'll take maybe two days, we were hoping for one." He started to pace the floor. "Let's see, they don't know about the oil truck yet. So what we do is hide this girl and her car. If they come, it will probably be late. We'll pretend that this is indeed a flying school and you all can act the part. After they leave, we can take her and her car and make it look like she had a car accident. All we need is three days. If we can keep them away that long, we're okay. I got word from the Homeland Security Office via the congressional committee just now that they found the M55 Rockets in Tooele. So we can't count on that diversion and then at the wedding I heard your precious Armad tell them about that stupid software blunder. They're going to start adding two and two." He shot a glance to Louise. "If that software glitch hadn't happened, we wouldn't have had to invent all those damn distractions!" He looked at Gabriel. "Your death, my Dear, will give us another day. We might be able to pull it off yet."

"You cannot get away with whatever it is you are doing. They will look for Armad and when they catch him, they will get him to tell them everything." Gabriel shouted at Andrews.

He started to laugh, an ugly laugh. "Gabriel, you are a little fool. You don't know a damn thing about what we're doing and neither does Armad. Right now he couldn't tell them if he did know!"

"Why not?" Then hesitatively, "He's dead?" Gabriel whispered more a fearful statement then a question.

Andrews, his face now livid, yelled at Louise. "If you hadn't told him about the flying lessons we wouldn't be in this mess now!"

"I had to tell him something! How else could I get away and teach these jerks to fly?" She screamed back.

Andrews started to pace again. "Of course, there is another plan. We could get Davis and Manning out here to rescue Gabriel and get rid of them. That would give us more time."

"Where is Moore, still on his honeymoon?" Louise was standing at the counter loading a gun into her purse.

"Unfortunately, Richard Moore is out in Tooele. It was he, or rather his little group, who figured out where the rockets were. They've captured Dowell, but at least he can keep his mouth shut. Everything is circumstantial and we can hire some good lawyers to get him out of anything they arrange. Of course we'll have to do away with him once we get him out. Damn, we had planned it so well. Then that stupid computer glitch when they hooked up the new program at the exact time as the switch was made between the oil tanker and the VX container. Damn! Nobody knew they were going to redo the software or if they did know could have predicted the timing! Too damn many things to keep track of! We fed that nerd Dudley a list of missing weapons that he could get them to go after and get them off the track. Then he had to go clever and start figuring the big picture! So we had to erase him! Damn! Such a beautifully simple plan mucked up!" Andrews swore.

"You killed John's friend, Dudley, too? He told me about it. He was heartbroken. Why?" Gabriel whispered.

"I just told you. Like you, he got nosey. Anyway, I didn't kill him. Dowell was our man on the scene for that. Stupid fool, damn near got himself killed by Moore's car when he went back in his army jeep to check at Davis's house to see if Dudley had made it there. The oaf could have called the hospital or his home! I'm surrounded by incompetents!" When Louise bristled, he smiled, "I didn't mean you, my dear. What would I have done without you to handle all the flying?" He raised his eyebrow and added, "But I must say leaving your cell-phone gun in Dudley's office when you bugged his phone was not the brightest thing you've ever done." Ignoring her, he turned to the young men. "Now, let's review the plan."

Louise motioned to Gabriel. "Aren't we forgetting something here? Small pitchers have wide ears."

"Why worry? She's not going anywhere and we can't let her out of our sight. Anyway, she'll be longtime dead by the time everything is done. Here's what we'll do. When Davis and Manning come, we'll go with the honest flying school story and hide little Miss Muffet here and her car. If they don't buy it, we'll just have to erase them." Gabriel shivered at the cold ease of his voice. *Oh God! This is like my ordeal in London! It all is happening again. Richard saved me then, but he's in Utah. Maybe, John?*

"We'll run over everything one more time. The oil truck will be delivering the VX tonight. The chemistry guys will come to the lab later tonight. They plan to prepare the nerve agent loaded in the ton container for spraying, move it into especially prepared tanks to load on your planes. Remember, stay away from the lab in the hanger when they are working. This is lethal stuff. Do you all have those special suitings I got for you?" The three nodded. "Good, remember, you put them on and don't take them off until you land and get out of the plane. So let's review what your instructions are. Ben?"

The shortest young man recited as if in a classroom, "As soon as the stuff is loaded I head up to Philadelphia and follow the written flight directions in the plane. Since I have a large flying-time gas supply I can cover a good deal of the area."

The other young man piped up, "I first do Washington then head up to Baltimore. Why aren't we doing New York?"

"Don't be silly. Everyone is watching New York skies after 9-11," Louise sneered.

Something is wrong, Gabriel thought. *They are reciting lines, but the body language seems to say they are spoofing the dialog, trying to con someone? Who? Certainly not me, I am just barely beginning to understand what's going on. Which one of them is being conned?*

"And they're not watching Washington?" Ben laughed. Andrews shot Louise a warning look.

Why they'll both be shot down! Gabriel grasped the situation faster then the young men involved seemed to. *Could they be so brain washed that they don't see their own demise? But then there are suicide bombers. But these guys will be wearing protective suits so they really think they will survive! Something doesn't add up here, something is off*!

The young man continued, "Then we come back here, put our suits in the bags and burn them and set fire to the planes! When do we get paid? You said after the attack we're to meet in San Francisco, but how will we get there? I've been thinking, all planes will be grounded?"

"My dear boy, have you never heard of the train? A car will be here and you simply drive to the station. " Louise interjected.

"What about you, Miss Know-it All? Where do you head? We keep hearing about our jobs but yours seems to be discussed in private with the mastermind here! As well as other things I might add." Ben scowled.

In a lofty tone, Louise answered, "I will head for Chicago. Since timing is important, and I can handle a plane better then you two, I'm going the farthest. Timing is paramount here. As soon as the first alert is sounded, planes will be going all over trying to find us. That's the advantage here. We can fly two meters off the ground, so we'll be hard to spot."

As they were concentrating on their conversation, Gabriel kept moving her chair closer to the door. *If I can just reach that dead bolt on the door and run for the car*, she thought. She waited for just the right time then jumped up and ran. Unfortunately, at that moment Andrews had turned his head and saw her. He grabbed her by the hair even as her hand was on the lock and pulled her toward him. She could feel his breath on her cheek. "Nice try! I see the French have not lost their spirit, just their nerve!" She spat at him.

Then a plan began to form in her mind. She had seen a flicker of a look in his eyes as he'd held her. Just a moment, but his scan was filled with an animal desire. She glanced back and gave him that come-hither look she'd practiced before the mirror when she was thirteen. The exchange was not lost on the three men or Louise.

"You've got yourself a little spit-fire there, boss?" Ben chided.

"Why don't I take little Miss Hard-to-Handle over to the next building? I'm afraid we may be getting ourselves away from thinking about what we are suppose to do here." Louise took Gabriel by the arm.

"Wait! I suggest we tie her hands before we let her move outdoors." Andrews came to her and bound her hands with duct tape from the counter. At his touch, Gabriel gave him another side glance. "On second thought, maybe I should take her next door and you three can go on with your planning."

"You fool! Do you think I'd let you jeopardize this whole plan to satisfy your animal instincts?" Louise recognized the leers of the three men. "May I speak with you a moment?" With an imperial tone, she motioned to Andrews.

At that moment Gabriel realized that it was Louise, not Andrews, in charge of the whole plan. *The way she pulled him aside, her chiding. The leader was Louise! But of course it all fell into place. She could keep track of everything going on in Homeland Security and the congressional committee by her relations with Andrews and Beel, links to computer communications and the Homeland Security Committee. Maybe she'd seduced Dowell also, which would bring in the army.*

Gabriel whispered to the two men left behind, "Do you really think Louise and Andrews will let you live? First, as soon as a hit is reported, fighter planes will be all over. You'll be swamped. If by some miracle you survive that, getting to San Francisco will be bad. If your strikes go through, all traveling will be in shambles, planes and trains. Then if, and that's a big 'if,' you get to San Francisco, what guarantee do you have…"

Louise had come up behind her back and cut in, "Trying to discredit our master plan? Spread doubts? You're talking frantically about something you cannot comprehend." She laughed and spoke to the two men near Gabriel who had been listening to her intently, "Please, don't pay her any attention. She was so easily fooled she thought we were taking flying lessons." She looked at Gabriel. "To become crop dusters? Do you have any idea how much lessons cost? Or how much crop duster pilots make? These guys know where the real money is. This child has no idea of the world; she's just trying to save her skin. I'm going to take her next door. She's nothing but a trouble maker." She pulled Gabriel to her feet and pushed her ahead out the door. "Move!"

The early darkness of late fall had descended. Only the outside lights of the hanger and the two buildings shone in a sea of blackness. Gabriel was surprised how strong Louise's hands were. One circled her arm like a vice. With the other hand Louise pushed open the door and turned on the light of the smaller of the two buildings. "There's a chair. Sorry I can't offer you coffee." Louise laughed.

At that moment Gabriel changed from a spirited girl to a strong women. She'd heard of born-again experiences but had laughed. Somewhere deep inside she felt her confidence burst forth. The feeling was so decided she felt that if she lived through this night, she would always call that her awaking. "Those two men are fools. Andrews is not the mastermind here, the boss! You are!" Gabriel turned to face Louise.

"I can see I've underestimated you. You're not the empty headed little flirt I thought. Since you won't be here very much longer, yes, I am the boss as you put it. What these fools can't see is that they are all expendable! Most men are!" Louise's eyes had narrowed. "When I was in college I waited tables to earn extra money. Once when I was serving the president's table, his wife came over and whispered something in his ear. Then a few minutes later he got up and made a remark complimenting an employee. I overheard a lady at another table say, 'She tells him what to say in such a nice way.' And she laughed. Every time I waited tables after that I watched her tell him what to say to whom. The president was a robot! That was the first time I realized many women, unlike my mother, were the born rulers, a turning point for me.

"My mother came from India. She did everything my father told her to. He was very cruel to her and …to me, in ways you could not imagine and I cannot bring myself to describe. My mother never defended either herself or me. I suffered both at home and then at school, the girls whispering about me and making fun of me. I vowed to get even with them all."

Gabriel interrupted, "But I was listening. No way can everything be done that Andrews said. You can't overnight make a dangerous liquid into a substance to discharge from airplanes. I studied and have degrees in chemistry as well as art at University." As she spoke Gabriel looked around the room for means of escape. *Keep Louise talking,* she thought. *I need to gain time*.

Louise scoffed, "Andrews is a fool! When the tank of VX was switched for oil in July it was taken to a secret lab in Tennessee and the contents altered to a less viscous substance suitable for spraying from the crop dusting planes. Trained technicians worked six weeks night and day to make the change. Several people died from contamination due to careless handling. You can't mix VX with water or alcohol, the reaction would destroy VX. They mixed it with a light grade machine oil. Then the VX-prepared solution was divided into six separate tanks, two for each plane. These tanks were loaded back into a larger oil truck that had been converted to hold them and returned to Indiana. Only an idiot would think you could do all that in two days. Also, we need to fly at altitudes of 300 to 500 feet so the spray will spread out over a large area. If we flew too close to the ground it would scare people and just fall in a smaller area.

"He's wrong about the timing of attack, also. We're going to leave at daybreak not at night. More people will be out and about in the daytime. We will make more hits. Andrews will be walking to work or maybe in his office when Ben sprays Washington. That is if he makes it to his office. We'll have someone waiting for him at his apartment."

"You mean those two men know that you're lying to Andrews?" The awful fact that Rene, Chloe, John and Richard would also be in Washington began to take hold in Gabriel's mind.

"But of course! They were just play-acting for Andrews benefit. The three of us were all trained in the same terrorist camp." Louise took great pleasure in Gabriel's surprise. "What those two fools don't know is that I'll be spraying New York! That's right, everyone will think we won't strike twice at one city. I've not only fooled Andrews but those two swaggering fools I taught to fly! We will probably all be dead before our planes hit the ground. I'll just enter Nirvana a little early! Men are such fools!"

"But I thought you said your mother was from India. Aren't the terrorist groups all Middle East Muslims?"

"Don't be silly. At my camps they trained young people from all over: Saudi Arabia, Turkey, the Philippines, Africa, China and yes, the United States. Once again, the women were more intelligent then the men. I must say, not all women were up to the training. Some are sheep like my mother." She hissed the word.

She's insane, Gabriel thought. *She has some kind of warped mind. She has lost all reason. I'll have to humor her*. So she asked, "Do you really think no one knows of your involvement? Aren't you concerned that the government may have asked for outside help?"

"You mean from the Noir? Oh don't look surprised. I know everything that goes on in that little committee. The Noir came in too late. I will say they have done a great deal of harm to our cause in a short time. I might add I have great admiration for Chloe Manning. She seems to be the cohesive force in that group. Now if she were working with us, we wouldn't need those morons. I do hope it never comes down to a battle between her and me. Although she is an opponent I would love to battle. Perhaps you've inherited some of her ability." Louise sat down in the chair opposite Gabriel and for the first time smiled.

"You look so much like Richard Moore. Makes me think maybe…" when she saw Gabriel blush and bristle. Louise laughed,… "I was right. I knew somewhere there was some connection! Ah the French! Is he your father? When did you find out?"

In spite of herself, Gabriel felt drawn to answer, "Just two days ago. I was crushed when I heard. I felt betrayed!" Why was she saying this? She felt disloyal to all those who had loved her, but she must gain time, make Louise talk more.

Louise smiled. "You realize that I'll have to shoot you. The little plan Andrews was pacing the floor expanding with is so full of holes you could pour water through it. The plan we will follow is very simple. We'll shoot you and then anyone who comes here looking for you. I give them an hour to realize you're gone. Then Bang! Bang!"

With a look of genuine respect, Louise continued, "You have comprehended this plan very quickly. Chemistry degree, you say, and art? Strange combination." Louise observed, "You seem like a nice little French girl. Really sorry it worked out this way. I think you would have done well in our camps. Now if you were some of those WASPS that used to rag me, I'd shoot them without a moment's hesitation. I can hear them now, 'your mother wears a sari. Did she get it from a sorry salesman?' and then giggle." She raised her gun.

CHAPTER TWELVE

"You are worried about Gabriel being gone? Don't worry, she's a good driver and knows you are counting on her to be home for the late dinner." Rene smiled.

"Rene, the reason we are worried is that this Armad and Louise that she was going to meet, well they may not be desirable people for her to know," John confessed.

"Then why did you introduce them to Gabriel? You say you care for her, why put her in jeopardy?" he demanded

"Rene, we were not sure. John tried to dissuade her from having anything to do with them. You know Gabriel does not like to be told what to do. Armad may be a fine young man. It's just that some things make us suspicious of him," Chloe amended.

"I think you had better tell me all about this situation. I have a right to know why these people are under suspicion. I am her father!" he bellowed.

"I will make this as succinct as I can, The U.S. government notified the Noir…"

"My God, not that stupid Noir again. Hasn't my family suffered enough from them. Surely Gabriel is not involved in anything to do with them?" Rene smoldered.

"Please just listen. The government asked us to check on some mix-up of numbering records on their chemical warfare records. It's sticky for one military group to check on another and they certainly wouldn't want another government to do it! They said everything was accounted for, they just found a confusion of numbers! So Noir said we would check. It turned out that Dudley Curtis on the same committee to check the numbers as John, Richard and myself was killed. We believe it was to hide some information. It also looks like some chemical weapons were stolen. This is very secret material and we are trusting your discretion." When Rene started to speak, Chloe raised her hand, "Wait, hear me out. We have recovered two of the three groups of chemical weapons that were stolen and Richard is on the track of the third group. In our investigation, we believe the weapons stolen were a diversion tactic from a larger threat. We believe that a ton container of VX has been stolen and terrorists are planning to deploy it. We don't know where. We think it may have some connection with those crop dusting lessons that Louise was talking so reluctantly about. The lessons Armad and Gabriel wanted to take."

"Mon Dieu! This business gets worse and worse. If ever I get Gabriel back, I will never bring her near you again!"

"Rene, you can not hide from these terrorists. If we don't stop them now, then they will surely do more harm. So far, our actions have avoided disastrous consequences, one in particular where thousands would have been killed. You cannot hide and you cannot make decisions for Gabriel. If what we believe to be true and what we are trying to avert would happen, Gabriel would be in danger even if she were nowhere near us. Right now I think we should be trying to decide what to do rather then arguing. Should we try and go to the flying lesson place or to the apartment where Louise and Armad live?" Chloe had begun pacing.

"I think we should try the apartment first! We know Armad was headed there and maybe Gabriel stopped there first. You sent out the wedding invitations, Chloe. Where is the list of invitation and addresses?" John demanded.

"I left the list in my room. Come upstairs and I'll get it. Rene, I suggest you come with us to Louise's. Nothing is worse then sitting and wondering what is happening." She hurried up the stairs as she spoke, went right to her desk and opened the wedding folder. "Here it is - on Massachusetts Ave. I'll call Harriet to get in touch with Richard. Last time I tried to reach him at Tooele his cell phone didn't work."

"I've already called Harriet and told her to give him a message. I'll get the car. Bring the address for the flying school with you. By the way, I also told Harriet of the result of a call from Matthews. He had his men working on full alert to test the contents of the one-ton containers in question and he got the results quickly. One of the tanks had oil in it. He got the license number of the truck that delivered the oil the day in question and now probably contains the VX. Thank God they keep such close records! I've called Colonel Green at Aberdeen and asked that the Army as well as the state police check all roads for that truck. I just hope to high heavens they are using the same truck. Green's contacting the Maryland and Virginia State Police. It's about a thirty-five minute drive to Louise's place. Hurry!"

When John parked the car near Wisconsin; they could hear the bells of the National Cathedral tolling in descending tones, a mournful sound. John remembered in Russia, for a death, the bells always went down one note at a time. Chloe shivered unconsciously. "Rene, we don't know what we are going to find. I know you'll want to come with us, but please stay back when we go in. Please?"

Rene nodded. They approached a four-story building of tan brick, an uninteresting block of modern mediocrity, each window like every other, doors that neither welcomed nor repelled. "It will be on the third floor. Please no talking. I'll ring the bell and then stand back. Rene, keep out of sight." They waited for the elevator in silence. No sound came from any of the apartments. Probably most of the occupants had jobs and were at work. Chloe rang the apartment bell and they waited. No answer. She rang again and then tried the handle, the door swung open. Back to back, she and John entered the living room. Nothing. The bedroom door was ajar and they silently made their way to it. They heard a slight groan. Slumped on the floor was Armad, surrounded by pools of blood.

"My Lord!" Chloe knelt beside him but addressed John, "Call 911!" Then to Armad, "Don't move. Help will be here soon." John went in the other room to phone. Rene looked on in horror. "Can you tell us what happened? How long have you been here?"

"I don't know," he tried to remember. "I guess I've passed out. I stopped by to pick up Louise and surprise her. I'd found the location of her airfield. I was going to take her out there with Gabriel. I thought she'd be pleased we cared enough to learn with her." He coughed. "I came in and found her in bed with Andrews. I couldn't believe it! She laughed!" He coughed again.

"I kept asking her why, but she just laughed. She was wearing that blue nightgown I had gotten her for her birthday. Andrews was buck-naked. He just got up and sneered. "You stupid fool. Can't you see? She's doing it for revenge, but I'm doing it for money. More money then I could ever get from this half-baked government job."

Armad coughed but kept on talking feverishly. "I asked, 'Did you kill that Dudley?' and Andrews spat. 'Hell no, I don't do minion stuff. Dowell did him in and then almost got clobbered by Moore when he went by the house to see if Dudley was dead. Talk about stupid! He could have called the hospital or his house. Then Andrews said, 'we can't leave him here. He knows too much.' And just like that, he took a gun from the bedside table and shot me. I guess I passed out. Have I been here long?"

"Passing out probably saved your life. They took you for dead. They must be pressed for time. Otherwise two hardened cases like Louise and Andrews would have made sure you were dead. Do you know where they went?" Chloe questioned.

"No." He slumped over again.

Chloe heard voices in the next room and John explaining, "He's in here. We found him just now." He followed two ambulance emergency men into the bedroom.

The driver spoke over his shoulder, “Lucky for you we were in the neighborhood when we got your call. We’d just delivered an old man home from the hospital.” He knelt beside Armad.

“He’s lost a lot of blood. We’ve got to get him to the hospital right away. He’s shallow breathing and a weak pulse, probably blood loss. The wound’s in the upper right arm. Probably hit a large vein. You start oxygen and I’ll put a tight pressure dressing over this bleeding area,” the ambulance driver talked as he worked while his assistant was adjusting the oxygen mask. “Get an IV started in his other arm so we can get some saline in to get his blood pressure up.” He looked up at Chloe. “Three things can get a man back to consciousness: raise the blood pressure, get in sugar and oxygen. The police will be here directly and get your names and all the info.” Then to his assistant in white “Get the stretcher ready.”

John protested, “We can’t wait here for the police. We’ve got to get to that airfield before. ...“ his cell phone rang and he flipped it open.

“Davis? Matthews here. We got the oil truck with the VX. They found it on I-95 outside of Stafford, Virginia about ten miles from Fredericksburg. A Colonel Green out of Aberdeen has them in custody and is questioning them. I really owe you one for this. I know we’re going to have feds crawling all over the place but it could be worse, a lot worse.”

“Do they know any names yet of anyone at the destination? Have the men in the truck contacted anyone?” John was breathing heavily.

“Nope, just got the call that they’d picked it up.” His voice was faint.

“Thanks, Keep me informed if you hear anything.” John looked at Rene and Chloe. “They found the truck and it’s secure. Look. I’m not going to wait for the police. I’m going out to that airfield right now. It’ll be a fifty-mile drive. Louise and Andrews don’t know yet that the truck has been stopped, unless the guys driving called. So if we can get there before they find out, we just might make it in time!”

Rene didn’t ask in time for what, he knew that Gabriel’s chance of survival would be for them to get there before news of the truck capture did. As they hurried toward the elevator, Chloe pointed out, "They are doing construction on Massachusetts at 7th Street. I'll guide you." They heard the police sirens coming down the street just as they got in the car and drove off.

"At 7th street you turn left onto I Street NW briefly, then right to get back to Massachusetts. At the roundabout take the second exit back to Massachusetts then…"she was talking rapidly and excitedly.

"I know, Chloe. Just let me drive! Cool it!" John interrupted.

Rene reached up from the back seat and put a reassuring hand on her shoulder. She reached back and covered his hand with a squeeze. *What a kind man he is*, she thought. *Gabriel's in danger again and it's all my fault!*

She watched the street signs as they went from US-50 to US –1 to I-395 and saw the 'Entering Virginia' sign then on to I-95. She felt as though she could physically feel the miles dragging away under her feet.

When they got to the turnoff to US-17 John suggested, "Rene, Gabriel said you were in the French resistance for a while and were a crack shot. Would you be willing to use a gun here? I have a spare in my briefcase in the back seat right beside you. Cartridges are in a box beside it."

"Bon, of course," Rene agreed.

They could hear him rustling around in the briefcase and then the click of cartridges being loaded. Ahead was a small sign 'airfield' with an arrow pointing to a dirt road on the right. John turned in and doused the lights. Ahead they could see two lighted- buildings to the right and an airplane hanger off to the left. "I think we better leave the car here and hoof it. Don't want to signal our coming."

Each one quietly exited the car and began the walk toward the buildings keeping to the shadows of the trees along the road. Through the windows, they could see two men with their backs toward them and Andrews standing at a table that had a paper sack with what looked like take-out food. They were all drinking coffee. In the building to their right they saw Gabriel sitting in a chair facing Louise.

"This is going to be tricky," whispered John. "We're going to have to hit both places at the same time. If we go in one building and rescue Gabriel, we're sitting ducks for the ones in the other building. If we get those three, we could sacrifice Gabriel. Rene, you and I can take those three. Chloe, you go for Gabriel. Don't worry, Rene, she's a better shot then either of us. We'll go to that door on the back of the building. Wait for my signal and we'll all go in at once." He crept away with Rene close behind.

Tiptoeing to the window of the building before her, Chloe heard Louise observing, "You seem like a nice little French girl. Really sorry it worked out this way. I think you would have done well in our camps. Now if you were some of those WASPS that used to rag me, I'd shoot them without a moment's hesitation. I can hear them now, 'your mother wears a sari. Did she get it from a sorry salesman?' and then giggle." She raised her gun. Chloe kept her eyes on John.

"I understand how you feel. My friends always used to whisper, 'so why doesn't she look like her mama or papa?' I hated it," Gabriel recalled. Chloe gasped thinking to herself, *Gabriel knew something was not as she had been told. All that time and she never mentioned it to anyone. So that's why she loved Richard. She wanted to escape. She thought she'd create her own safe little family.*

Chloe raised her gun and approached the door, eyes on John. When he lifted his hand she struck the door open with her foot and fired at the same time that the startled Louise swung her gun around and fired, the shots so close, they sounded like one large explosion. Louise had a surprised look on her face as she slumped to the floor and crumpled over the gun in her hand. Since Louise was not facing her, Chloe had aimed for Louise's head, just above the left ear. When Louise turned the bullet had hit her right between the eyes. Gabriel heard several shots from the building next by but paid no attention. She had eyes only for the still figures on the floor. She tried to jump up and run to Chloe who was lying on her side just inside the door but Gabriel's legs and feet seemed to have heavy weights attached to them. She was pushing each of her feet onto the floor, one ahead of the other. Everything was moving in agonizing slow motion. As if viewing the room from a distance she saw John burst in and shout, "We got them!" Finally Gabriel reached Chloe and she knelt beside her. From a point to the side of Chloe's left temple, blood was flowing onto Gabriel's hand and dress as she knelt beside her. When Louise turned she must have caught Chloe on the side of the head, a lucky hit. For a moment Gabriel stared at the blood pooling around her and then the quiet, limp body of her grandmother lying in her arms. She screamed and the sound bounced off the walls, echoing through the empty room. "**NO**!"

Absently mindedly, Richard drummed his fingers on the arm of the sofa as he contemplated the rain splattering on the windows and then moved his eyes to gaze on a small, silver-framed photo of Chloe on the end table. Harriet, who had been watching the flame blazing in the fireplace turned to watch him. Worry, exhaustion and sadness were vying for control in his expression. She walked over to the sofa and settled beside him. "Would it help to talk?" she asked.

Slowly, he brought her face into focus. "What a waste! I still can't believe Chloe is gone. Her humor, knowledge, calmness in the midst of all this madness, all gone. I've worked with and depended on her for so long." He almost whispered. "I still can't believe it. If only I had gotten back sooner! Where is Gabriel?"

"Rene took her to John's house and I think she is under sedation. Rene didn't think she should go to the funeral or the cemetery. Poor Gabriel, she has had a hard time these last few years. Although, John and Rene are approaching burn-out, too." She took his hand in hers to stop the fingers drumming. "What will happen to them…Gabriel and John, I mean?"

"My Dear, I have no idea. Gabriel needs a long rest and John is determined to keep her safe. He's even more rabid than Rene on the subject, if that's possible. God, but I miss Chloe! She was always such a rock, always there with a solution! Calm, clever, deliberate."

Harriet stroked his hand and said, "Jo Ferguson called. She's been with Jack Bancroft all through his surgery. She said she's taking him to her folks home in Michigan as soon as he can travel. She said to tell you Armad is leaving the government and taking a job with IBM. What's happened to the missing chemical weapons and the chemical containers? Have they all been recovered?"

"Yes, all are secure and accounted for, but as long as any remain either in military custody, buried or unknown, they will be a magnet to any terrorist group in the world. Our only hope is to get rid of them. The argument continues between scientific groups about the 'right' way to demolish the weapons and chemicals. Then there are the media groups, some want to alert the public to the dangers and others want to scare and sensationalize the situation. Even if we get rid of every last bit, the Russians had 80,000,000 pounds of chemical weapons, stuff that'll draw terrorists like bees to honey. So far the Russians only demolished 3%, costly business this demolition and the Russians need money."

The phone ringing broke the silence. Harriet reached for the receiver. "Don't answer it!" Richard put his hand over hers. "Come to bed. I'm tired of the whole damn business and I want some loving."

"But it could be important!"

"Probably is. They can just go to hell!"

READING GROUP QUESTIONS AND TOPICS FOR DISCUSSION

1. After reading this book, do you think the media has exaggerated the subject of chemical weapons?

2. Which method of chemical weapon destruction do you favor? Why?

3. Should information concerning the army bases where chemicals are stored be available on the Internet? Why?

4. Should the government call in a foreign undercover agency to check on one of its services? If not, how should a suspicious situation be handled?

5. Do you, or do you know someone who lives near one of the army bases mentioned? Should more precautions be used? What?

6. In the construction of the book, what was the most important: character development? Plot development? Getting information on chemical weapons across?

7. Do you think a main character should die? Why or why not?

8. If you were stealing chemical weapons, what method would you use?

9. A parallel exists between the personal lives of the characters working to abort the theft of weapons and the characters intent on stealing the weapons. Can you identify the relationships?

10. Have you any experience with mustard agent, or know someone who has? Any other kind of chemical poisoning?

11. In case of a chemical attack, what would you do?

ABOUT THE AUTHOR

This is Murray's third Noir mystery. The first was The Chinese Treasure. Her second, A Pox on You, won first prize in fiction from Delaware Press Women and second place from the National Federation of Press Women. Murray has also published non-fiction articles in Delaware Today and the Philadelphia Inquirer. Murray did graduate work in biology at the University of Michigan and research work at the Oak Ridge National Laboratory. She lives with her husband in the college town of Newark, Delaware.

Printed in the United States
24739LVS00005B/246